B180 Basketball Fundamental Skills Program

Basketball Coaches and Personal Trainers: The Definitive Guide to Improving Player Development and Earning More

DAVID SMITH

B180 Basketball, Inc
P.O. Box 2406
Midland, MI 48641-2406
www.b180basketball.com
Phone: 1-800-957-1275

© 2017 by David Smith. All rights reserved.

No part of this book may be reproduced, stored in a retrieval system, or transmitted by any means without written permission of the author.

Published by B180 Basketball, Inc. 1/19/2018

ISBN: 9780692317617 (sc)
ISBN: 9780692306666 (e)
ISBN: 978-0-692-09739-7 (hc)

Library of Congress Control Number: 2018900661

Any persons depicted in stock imagery are models and such images are being used for illustrative purposes only.

Because of the dynamic nature of the Internet, any web addresses or links contained in this book may have changed since publication and may no longer be valid. The views expressed in this work are solely those of the author and do not necessarily reflect the views of the publisher, and the publisher hereby disclaims any responsibility for them.

DEDICATION

This book is dedicated to all of my family members past, present, and future. My heart, soul, and passion has always been basketball. My message to the next generation of Smith's: Remember to follow your passion and bring your dream to life. Stay far away from negative individuals, things, situations, and places. Help others along your journey. Read your bible, believe, and give your absolute best in all endeavors. Never give up. I love, trust, and believe in you.

ACKNOWLEDGMENTS

I'd like to acknowledge my elementary librarian Mrs. Lynn Dent, my parents David & Connie Smith, my grandmother Lula B. Smith, my uncle Terry Smith, and all of my coaches Jimmy Sanders, Steve Schmidt, Dean Lockwood, and Bob Taylor. Thank you for molding me into the individual that I've become and will be. You were there when I needed you most and you gave me your best. I am grateful for everything that you have taught me and your encouragement for me to be a lifelong learner.

Contents

Welcome 1

Effort & Challenge Oath 2

Safety Statement 3

Overview 5

Glossary 6

Calendar 9

Chapter 1: Skills Test 12

Chapter 2: Spot Skill Development 26

Chapter 3: Pure Shooting 33

Chapter 4: Perimeter & Post Footwork 40

Chapter 5: Defense & Free Throws 52

Chapter 6: Ball Handling Wisdom 63

Chapter 7: Footwork & Ball Handling 76

Chapter 8: Level II Spot Skill Development 87

Chapter 9: Level II Perimeter & Post Footwork 98

Chapter 10: Level II Ball Handling Wisdom 109

Chapter 11: Level II Pure Shooting 128

B180 BASKETBALL FUNDAMENTAL SKILLS PROGRAM

Welcome to the Basketball **B180** Fundamentals Skills Program

GET READY TO IMPROVE EVERY AREA OF YOUR BASKETBALL GAME

This is probably the most complete and challenging basketball workout program designed. If you feel that you can give your best and challenge yourself in every workout, B180 will work for you. The B180 Basketball Fundamental Skills Program was created to make you a better basketball player in just 60 days. Using basketball fundamental skill workouts that focus on details in ball handling, footwork, shooting, conditioning, and defense, you will experience firsthand what it takes to become an elite basketball player.

In sixty days you will be a better basketball player. You will have basketball confidence, skills, and conditioning. While you may be pushed to the limits after some workouts, you'll feel an extreme sense of confidence in your basketball abilities.

This is a challenging basketball workout program. You must give your best effort and challenge yourself to follow the workout completely and in order. Consult your physician before beginning this program.

Warning: IF YOU COMMIT TO B180, YOU WILL BE A BETTER BASKETBALL PLAYER. BUT YOU MUST BE WILLING TO CHALLENGE YOURSELF IN EVERY WORKOUT. YOU MUST CHECK WITH YOUR PHYSICIAN BEFORE STARTING THIS PROGRAM.

B180 BASKETBALL FUNDAMENTAL SKILLS PROGRAM EFFORT & CHALLENGE OATH

Before you begin the program to become a better basketball player, please read the following statement.

As an individual that plans to give my best effort and to challenge myself over the next 60 days, I understand that some workouts will challenge me. I will strive to be the best that I can be. I also understand that by completing the B180 Basketball Fundamental Skills Program I may gain a competitive advantage on some of my competition. If during or after completion of the program I choose to share the B180 Basketball Fundamental Skills Program information, I understand that I may be challenged to maintain the same competitive advantage on my competition.

If you agree:
(Optional)
Signed: _____ Date: _____

WARNING: The B180 Basketball Fundamental Skills Program is an intense and challenging workout. It is NOT for beginners or individuals with any medical condition that may be compromised by intense basketball training. Consult your physician before beginning this program.

Basketball Fundamentals Skills Program- Safety Statement

Before beginning any exercise program, you should see your health care provider for a physical and medical clearance. If you are using a personal trainer, be sure that the personal trainer you choose puts you through a comprehensive assessment to evaluate medical history, personal goals and look at your current physical status.

If you are not using a personal trainer, always begin and progress slowly. For a full understanding of your health status and general fitness before starting an exercise program, you should see your health care provider for a physical and medical clearance.

For safety and to prevent injuries before starting your fitness program, meet with a certified personal trainer for a dynamic postural assessment. A dynamic postural assessment observes your basic body movements, how your muscles and joints work together, and to look for any imbalances or dysfunctions in your posture alignment that can be corrected.

No matter which type of exercise you do, there are certain factors to consider each and every time you exercise. Below are suggestions that can help you stay safe while exercising.

- Check with your doctor before starting an exercise program.
- Set aside a specific time each day to make physical activity and exercise part of your routine so you are less likely to skip the workout.
- When needed, you can take a water break
- Get a friend or family member to assist you. This will make your physical activity more enjoyable, help you encourage each other, and it's the safest way to exercise.
- Always warm up for at least 5 to 10 minutes (or longer if you have special considerations such as heart disease or other medical conditions) before any physical activity and cool down at least 5 to 10 minutes at the end of your activity.
- If at any time you feel you are going beyond your current fitness abilities or feel lightheaded, dizziness, nausea, or chest discomfort during physical activity, call your doctor or dial 911 in the case of an emergency. You should discontinue the exercise immediately and reconsider your use of this routine in particular
- Wear comfortable shoes with good arch and ankle support.
- Wear comfortable clothing. No fancy workout garb required. A comfy t-shirt and shorts/sweats will do.
- It's a good idea to get a heart monitor so you can check the intensity of your workout and progress safely.
- If you exercise outside, workout in a safe, well-lit area.
- Stay well-hydrated. Keep the water bottle filled and handy.
- Rest when needed

DAVID SMITH

WARNING

All contents written in this program is protected under the copyright laws of the United States and other countries.

This written program is sold for individual use only and all other rights are expressly reserved by the owner of such written program. Any copying or public performance of such written program is strictly prohibited and may subject the offender to civil liability and severe criminal penalties. (Title 17, United States Code Section 501 and 506)

B180 Basketball Fundamentals Skills Program Overview

The B180 Basketball Fundamental Skills Program is a 60 day training program for individuals that want to improve their overall basketball skill level. David Smith, a former college head basketball coach created the program. Coach Smith also played college basketball. The program was created to enhance the overall basketball skill level of individuals. The B180 workouts can be done on an outdoors or indoors basketball court. The B180 program will challenge you to be a disciplined player as you complete the workouts. Below is what to expect over the next 60 days

Month 1
In the first month, a strong foundation built on basketball footwork, shooting, ball handling, and defense.

Month 2
In the second month, there is an enhanced focus on basketball footwork, shooting, and ball handling. In the second month you are challenged to create consistency to perform at an elite level

B180 Basketball Fundamental Skills Program Glossary

Baseline- The out of bounds area behind the basket

Breakdown into defensive stance 3/4 of the way- Before you get to a line or area, you stutter step or move feet quickly and under control slowing down into a low defensive stance

Center top of key 3pt area- Facing the basket, it's the center area above the free throw line and behind the 3pt line

Chest pass- Two handed pass from the center of your chest. Step forward when passing with your dominant foot

Defensive stance- With your back to the basket, body is low to the ground. Feet are shoulder length apart. One hand will be raised above your head. One hand will be extended out wide. Eyes will be looking at opponents eyes

Free throw line- Facing the basket, the center area below the 3pt line that normally has a straight line identifying the area

Front pivot left- A jump stop then turn (half circle) to the front moving your right foot forward and keeping your left foot planted

Front pivot right- A jump stop then turn (half circle) to the front moving your left foot forward and keeping your right foot planted

Half court- The center line that divides the full basketball court

High post areas- Facing the basket, the areas just below the free throw line between the right and left elbows

Jab step- using a quick step forward with the left or right foot. Then a quick step back

Jump hook- turning to the right or left and jumping off of both feet, then shooting the basketball with the right or left hand only

Jump stop- slightly jumping (not high in the air) and landing softly with your feet shoulder length apart and on balance

Left box out- While in a defensive stance with back to the basket, reverse pivot left; Stay low to the ground and have arms wide and extended out (you must raise hands above your head to get rebound)

Left block- Facing the basket, the area to the left that has a rectangle shape (always post up above the block between the first hash mark in the floor)

Left corner 3pt area- Facing the basket, the area to the left behind the 3pt line where the baseline and sideline meets

Left foot drop step- Moving the left foot backwards into a jump stop

Left hand behind the back dribble- While dribbling the basketball with your left hand, quickly wrap the basketball completely behind your back and in front of you again to your right hand

Left hand behind the back pass- Left hand dominated pass wrapping the basketball around your back as you make the pass

Left hand crossover dribble- While dribbling the basketball with your left hand, quickly dribble the basketball low over to your right hand in front of you

Left hand overhand layup- Shooting the basketball off the backboard and into the basket with the left hand only; hand is on top of the basketball while shooting

Left hand overhand shot- Shooting the basketball inside the high and low post areas with the left hand only; floating the basketball into the basket

Left hand pass- Left hand dominated pass from the left side of your chest and shoulder area. Step forward with your left foot when passing

Left hand spin dribble- While dribbling the ball with your left hand reverse pivot right; make a full turn with the basketball and push the ball out in front of youLeft short corner area- Facing the basket, the area near the baseline between the left block and the left corner 3pt area

Left wing 3pt area- Facing the basket, the area on the perimeter behind the 3pt line between the left corner 3pt area and the center top of key 3pt area

Low post areas- Facing the basket, the areas between the right & left block and in front of the basket

Opposite baseline- With your back to the basket near a baseline, the baseline that is at the other end of the full basketball court

Opposite free throw line- With your back to the basket near a baseline, the free throw line at the other end of the full basketball court

Overhead pass- Two handed pass from above and behind your head and shoulder area. Step forward with your dominant foot when passing

Pull up jump shot- While dribbling the basketball do a complete jump stop and shoot the basketball

Reverse pivot left- A jump stop then turn to the back (full circle) moving your right foot backwards and keeping your left foot planted

Reverse pivot right- A jump stop then turn to the back (full circle) moving your left foot backwards and keeping your right foot planted

Right box out- While in a defensive stance with back to the basket, reverse pivot right; Stay low to the ground and have arms wide and extended out (you must raise hands above your head to get rebound)

Right block- Facing the basket, the area to the right that has a rectangle shape (always post up above the block between the first hash mark in the floor)

Right corner 3pt area- Facing the basket, the area to the right behind the 3pt line where the baseline and sideline meets

Right foot drop step- Moving the right foot backwards into a jump stop

Right hand behind the back dribble- While dribbling the basketball with your right hand, quickly wrap the basketball completely behind your back and in front of you again to your left hand

Right hand behind the back pass- Right hand dominated pass wrapping the basketball around your back as you make the pass

Right hand crossover dribble- While dribbling the basketball with your right hand, quickly dribble the basketball low over to your left hand in front of you

Right hand overhand layup- Shooting the basketball off the backboard and into the basket with the right hand only; hand is on top of the basketball while shooting

Right hand overhand shot- Shooting the basketball inside the high and low post areas with the right hand only; floating the basketball into the basket

Right hand pass- Right hand dominated pass from the right side of your chest and shoulder area. Step forward with your right foot when passing

Right hand spin dribble- While dribbling the ball with your right hand reverse pivot left; make a full turn with the basketball and push the ball out in front of you

Right short corner area- Facing the basket, the area near the baseline between the right block and the right corner 3pt area

Right wing 3pt area- Facing the basket, the area on the perimeter behind the 3pt line between the right corner 3pt area and the center top of key 3pt area

Shot fake- Going through the motion of shooting the basketball but do not shoot it. Stay low to the ground and don't leave your feet (move your elbows up and down)

Stop & go- An almost complete stop, then a quick sprint take off or burst of speed

Stutter step- Quickly moving your feet together as if you are running in place

Basketball Fundamental Skills Program

Month 1: Put an "X" in each day you do your B180 workout

	Sunday	Monday	Tuesday	Wednesday	Thursday	Friday	Saturday
Week 1	Off	Skill Test	Spot Skill Development	Pure Shooting	Perimeter & Post Footwork	Defense & Free Throws	Ball Handling Wisdom
Week 2	Off	Pure Shooting	Defense & Free Throws	Spot Skill Development	Perimeter & Post Footwork	Pure Shooting	Ball Handling Wisdom
Week 3	Off	Skill Test	Spot Skill Development	Defense & Free Throws	Perimeter & Post Footwork	Pure Shooting	Ball Handling Wisdom
Week 4	Off	Defense & Free Throws	Pure Shooting	Spot Skill Development	Perimeter & Post Footwork	Defense & Free Throws	Ball Handling Wisdom

Footwork & Ball Handling Week

Off	Footwork & Ball Handling	Footwork & Ball Handling	Footwork & Ball Handling	Footwork & Ball Handling	Footwork & Ball Handling	Footwork & Ball Handling

Basketball Fundamental Skills Program

Month 2: Put an "X" in each day you do your B180 workout

	Sunday	Monday	Tuesday	Wednesday	Thursday	Friday	Saturday
Week 5	Off	Skill Test & Level II Spot Skill Development	Level II Ball Handling Wisdom	Level II Pure Shooting	Level II Perimeter & Post Footwork	Level II Spot Skill Development	Level II Ball Handling Wisdom
Week 6	Off	Level II Pure Shooting	Level II Spot Skill Development	Level II Ball Handling Wisdom	Level II Perimeter & Post Footwork	Level II Pure Shooting	Footwork & Ball Handling
Week 7	Off	Skill Test & Level II Spot Skill Development	Level II Ball Handling Wisdom	Level II Pure Shooting	Level II Perimeter & Post Footwork	Level II Spot Skill Development	Footwork & Ball Handling
Week 8	Off	Level II Ball Handling Wisdom	Level II Pure Shooting	Level II Spot Skill Development	Footwork & Ball Handling	Level II Ball Handling Wisdom	Level II Pure Shooting

	Sunday	Monday	Tuesday	Wednesday	Thursday	Friday	Saturday
Week 9	Off	Final Skill Test					

A Basketball Wish

As the stars light up the sky on a hot summer night
The sound that's heard causes some to take flight
With unwavering force it goes on and on
Many stare wondering when will it be done
Walk after walk and street after street
The challenge that's given is to not miss a beat
As the night grows old nobody's there
There's a pause in the road, along with a prayer
It all started with this so, I pass it with a no look dish
This.... Yes. This is my basketball wish.

By
David Carl Smith Jr.

Chapter 1

SKILLS TEST

Warm Up (Perform each movement by itself down the court and back)

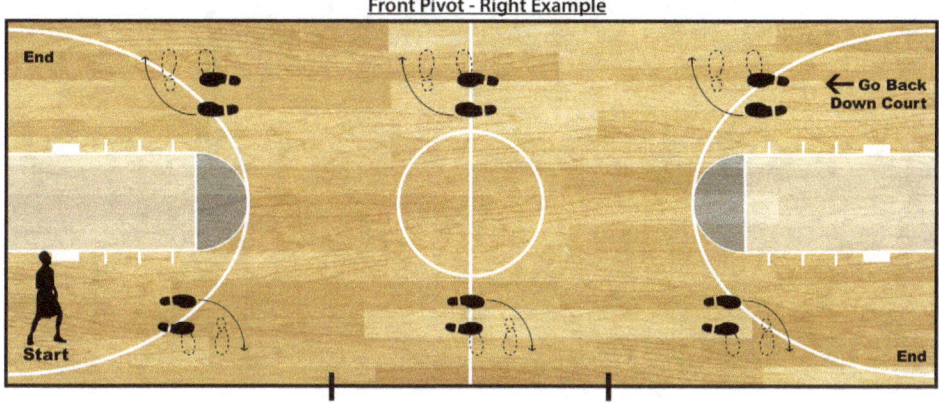

Note: All warm up workouts start at the baseline. Individuals should do movements asked at the *free throw line/half court line/ opposite free throw line/ opposite baseline*. Then repeat workout going back to your starting point.

Warm Up (perform each movement by itself down the court and back)

Jump Stop
Front Pivot Right
Front Pivot Left
Reverse Pivot Right
Reverse Pivot Left
Stutter Step
Stop and Go

Note: Perform the moves listed. Do as many repetitions as you can, then record your results after each workout. Remember to warm up and rest when needed. The B180 Basketball Fundamental Skills Program is a physically demanding workout. This is NOT for beginners or individuals with any medical condition that may be compromised by intense basketball training. Consult your physician and read the enclosed safety statement and other materials before beginning this program.

B180 BASKETBALL FUNDAMENTAL SKILLS PROGRAM

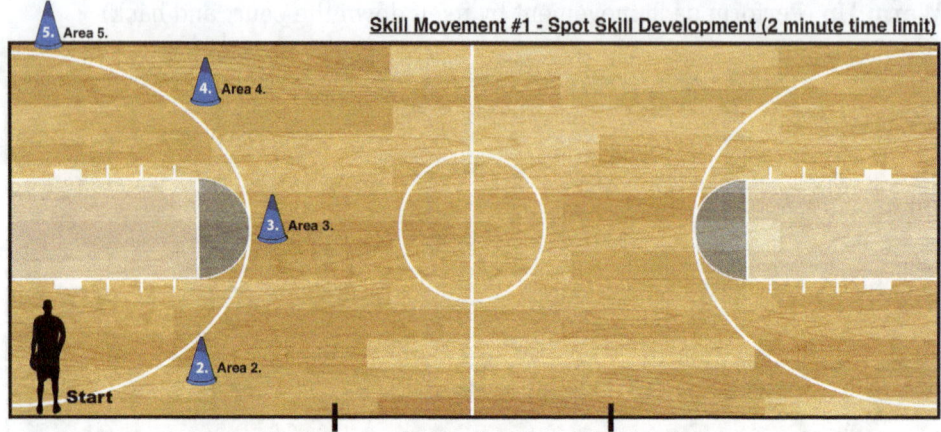

Start in the left corner behind the 3pt line. Locate the five (5) starting areas behind the 3pt line on the diagram. Go as quickly as you can to get your own rebound. In this workout always start your workout behind the three point line. Write down your results. Follow the sequence given below.

Skill Movement #1- Spot Skill Development (2 minute time limit)

Start in the left corner behind the 3pt line

1. Make a 3pt shot
2. Shot fake, (go left) 1 dribble towards basket & make a pull up jump shot
3. Shot fake, (go left) 1-2 dribbles towards basket & make a left overhand layup or shot
4. Shot fake, (go right) 1 dribble towards basket & make a pull up jump shot
5. Shot fake, (go right) 1-2 dribbles towards basket & make a right overhand layup or shot

Move to next spot on diagram and repeat movements above.

Results

Skill test #1 _____

Skill test #2 _____

Skill test #3 _____

Skill test #4 _____

Final Skill test _____

SKILLS TEST

Skill Movement #2 - Pull Back Full Court (1 minute time limit)

Repeat workout for 1 minute. Follow the directions for each task listed below before moving on. Locate the starting area on the diagram. Go as quickly as you can to get to the next area on the court. Place cones at the four (4) outside 3pt wing areas listed on the diagram. The movement sequence should go *dribble basketball to cone, breakdown into low stance 3/4 of the ways while dribbling the basketball low, slide at an angle back towards the basket, crossover and go forward, dribble to cone at the far end of the court, repeat movements again, dribble in to make a layup, go back down court repeating movements again.* In this workout always start your workout on the baseline near the left corner. Write down your results.

Follow the sequence given below.

Skill Movement #2-Pull Back Full Court (1 minute time limit)

Start on the baseline near the left corner

1. Run and dribble basketball with (right hand) to the cone, stay low and while facing forward, dribble back towards your starting point using 2 dribbles (left foot in front, eyes looking down court), crossover dribble the basketball in front of you. Then dribble forward down court in 4 dribbles.

See "Skill Movement #2 Continued- Pull Back Full Court" card

B180 BASKETBALL FUNDAMENTAL SKILLS PROGRAM

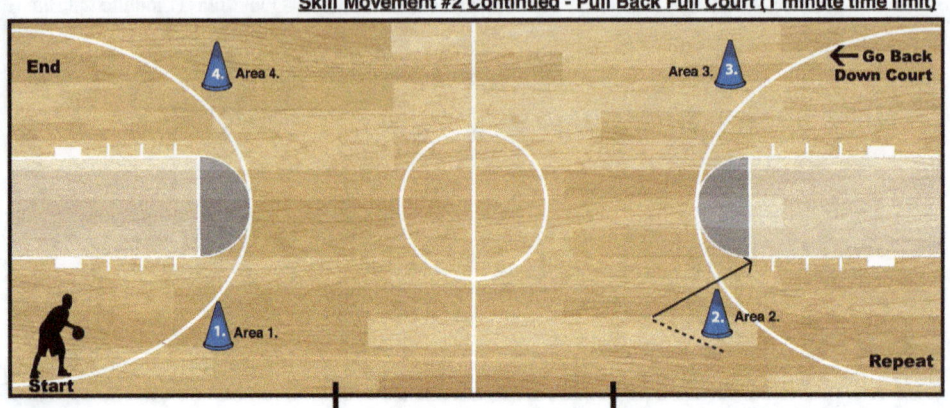

Skill Movement #2 Continued-Pull Back Full Court (1 minute time limit)

Start on the baseline near the left corner

2. Run and dribble basketball with (right hand) to the cone, stay low and while facing forward, dribble back towards your starting point using 2 dribbles (left foot in front, eyes looking down court), crossover dribble the basketball in front of you. Then dribble forward into the lane and make 1 overhand left hand shot.

Repeat movements above continuously for 1 minute going up and down both sides of the court (start in left corner at both ends of the court)

Results

Skill test #1 _____
Skill test #2 _____
Skill test #3 _____
Skill test #4 _____
Final Skill test _____

SKILLS TEST

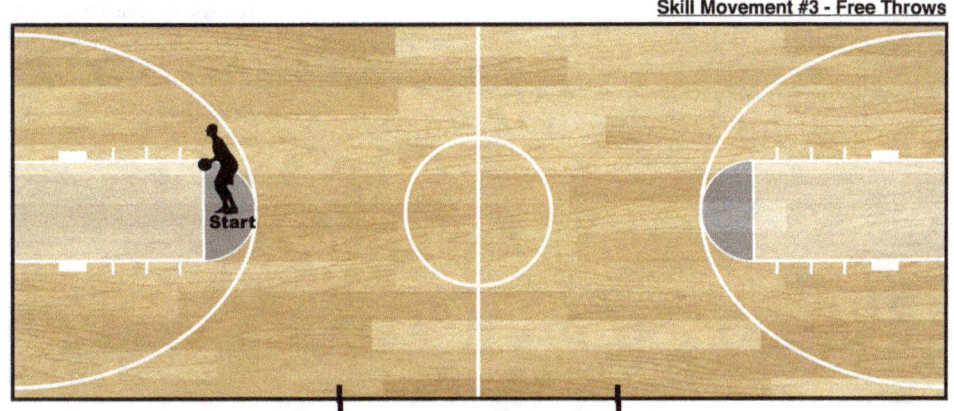

Skill Movement #3 - Free Throws

Start at the free throw line. Get your own rebound. Write down your results. Follow the directions given below .

Skill Movement #3-Free Throws
Start at the free throw line
1. Count how many free throws you can make consecutively in a row.

Results
Skill test #1 _____
Skill test #2 _____
Skill test #3 _____
Skill test #4 _____
Final Skill test _____

B180 BASKETBALL FUNDAMENTAL SKILLS PROGRAM

Skill Movement #4 Walking Dribble

Start on the baseline. Go as quick as you can. Write down your results

Follow the directions given below.

Skill Movement #4 Walking Dribble

Start on the baseline

2. Walk down court and dribble between the leg continuously (alternating with left & right hand). Count how many between the leg dribbles you complete without mishandling the basketball or losing your dribble. Go down the court and back

Results

Skill test #1 _____

Skill test #2 _____

Skill test #3 _____

Skill test #4 _____

Final Skill test _____

SKILLS TEST

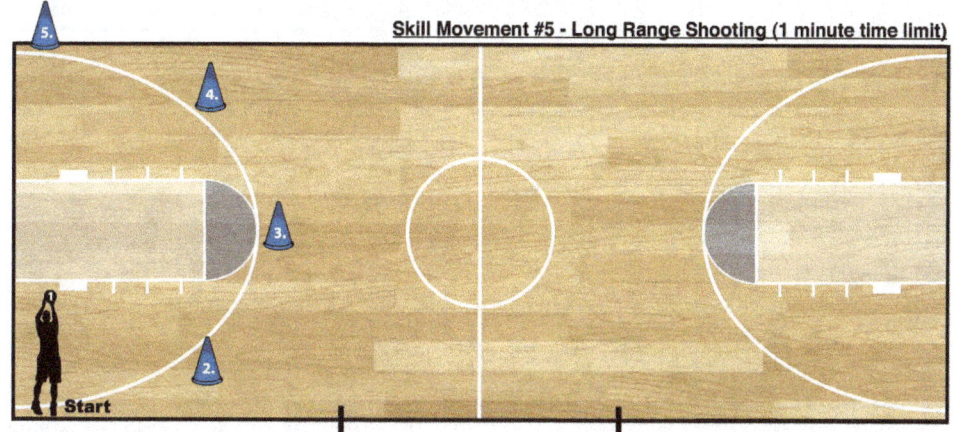

Start in the left corner behind the 3pt line. Locate the five (5) 3pt areas on the diagram. Go as quickly as you can to get your own rebound. No dribble is needed. The sequence should go *shoot basketball, sprint to get rebound, sprint back to area with the basketball and shoot the basketball again.* Remember no dribble is needed at any point just rebound, sprinting, and shooting. Write down your results

Follow the sequence given below.

Skill Movement #5-Long Range Shooting (1 minute time limit)

Start outside the 3pt line in the left corner

3. Make 5 jump shots from the left 3pt corner spot
4. Make 5 jump shots from the left 3pt wing spot
5. Make 5 jump shots from the center 3pt top of key spot
6. Make 5 jump shots from the right 3pt wing spot
7. Make 5 jump shots from the right 3pt corner spot

Results

Skill test #1 _____

Skill test #2 _____

Skill test #3 _____

Skill test #4 _____

Final Skill test _____

B180 BASKETBALL FUNDAMENTAL SKILLS PROGRAM

Skill Movement #6 - Perimeter Movement (2 minute time limit)

Start on left wing behind 3pt line. Locate the starting areas on the diagram. Go as quickly as you can to get your own rebound. No dribble is needed. The sequence should go *shoot basketball, sprint to get rebound, place basketball where it should be, sprint back to starting point, and repeat movements again*. Remember no dribble is needed unless directed in a movement. Basketball is placed on the ground at the ending point if you are doing the workout alone and you do not have a person to pass you the ball. Write down your results. Follow the sequence given below.

Skill Movement #6-Perimeter Movement (2 minute time limit)

Start out on the left wing behind the 3pt line

1. Run to right wing (foot touches the left & right blocks), run back down and touch right block again, run back to right wing, pick up the basketball and make one 3 pt. jump shot
2. Run to right wing (foot touches the left & right blocks), run back down and touch right block again, run back to right wing, pick up the basketball, shot fake, (go right) 1 dribble towards the basket, and make a jump shot

See "Skill Movement #6 Continued-Perimeter Movement" card

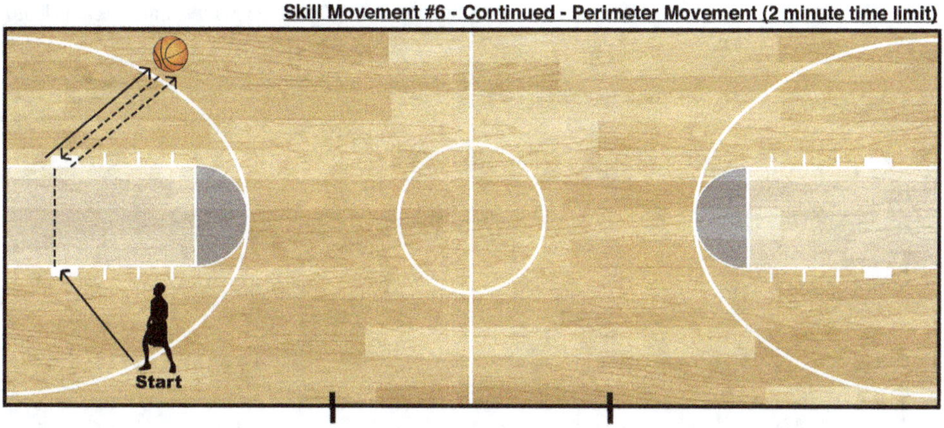

SKILLS TEST

Skill Movement #6 - Continued - Perimeter Movement (2 minute time limit)

Skill Movement #6 Continued-Perimeter Movement (2 minute time limit)

Start out on the left wing behind the 3pt line

3. Run to right wing (foot touches the left & right blocks), run back down and touch right block again, run back to right wing, pick up the basketball, shot fake, (go right) 1-2 dribbles, and make a right hand overhand layup

Results

Skill test #1 _____
Skill test #2 _____
Skill test #3 _____
Skill test #4 _____
Final Skill test _____

Repeat workout for 1 minute. Start on the baseline. Go as quickly as you can to get your own rebound. Write down your results.

Follow the sequence given below.

Skill Movement #7-Chasing Layups (1 minute time limit)

Start on the baseline

1. Run while dribbling (alternate left & right hand) the basketball using 4-5 dribbles down court to the other basket and make a right hand overhand layup. Get your rebound
2. Run while dribbling (alternate left & right hand) the basketball using 4-5 dribbles down court to the other basket and make a right hand overhand layup. Get your rebound

Repeat movements for 1 minute

Results

Skill test #1 _____
Skill test #2 _____
Skill test #3 _____
Skill test #4 _____
Final Skill test _____

SKILLS TEST

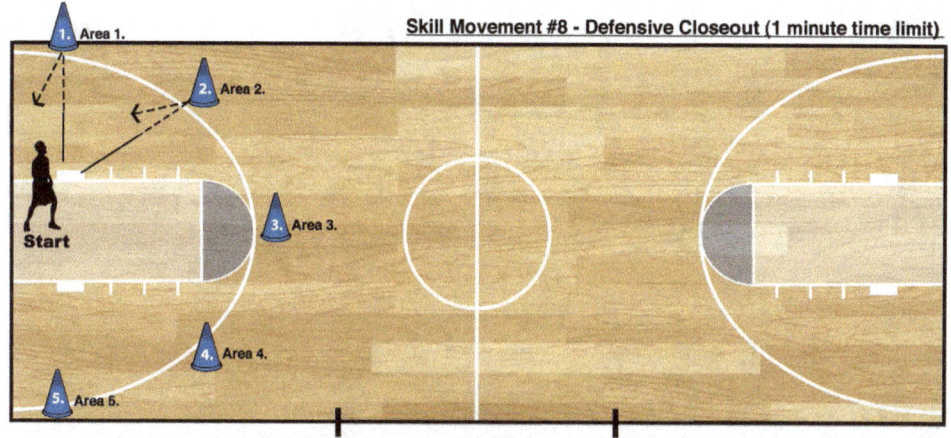

Repeat workout for 1 minute. Follow the directions for each task listed below before moving on to a different area. Locate the starting area on the diagram. Go as quickly as you can to get to the next area on the court. Place cones around the 3 pt. line in the five (5) areas listed on the diagram. The movement sequence should go *run out to the cone, breakdown into defensive stance 3/4 of the ways to 3 pt. line, slide at an angle back towards the basket, go back to starting point, and repeat movements again.* In this workout always start your workout near the basket in the middle of the lane. Write down results for how many times you get around the entire perimeter.

Follow the sequence given below.

Skill Movement #8-Defensive Closeout (1 minute time limit)

Start out underneath the basket in the middle of the lane.

1. Run out to left corner 3 pt. line, break down in defensive stance 3/4 of way with right foot in front and right hand high, stay in defensive stance and slide (go left) back towards basket between the left block and baseline.

2. Run out to left wing 3 pt. line, break down in defensive stance 3/4 of way with right foot in front and right hand high, stay in defensive stance and slide (go left) back towards basket to the left block

See 'Skill Movement #8 Continued-1" card

B180 BASKETBALL FUNDAMENTAL SKILLS PROGRAM

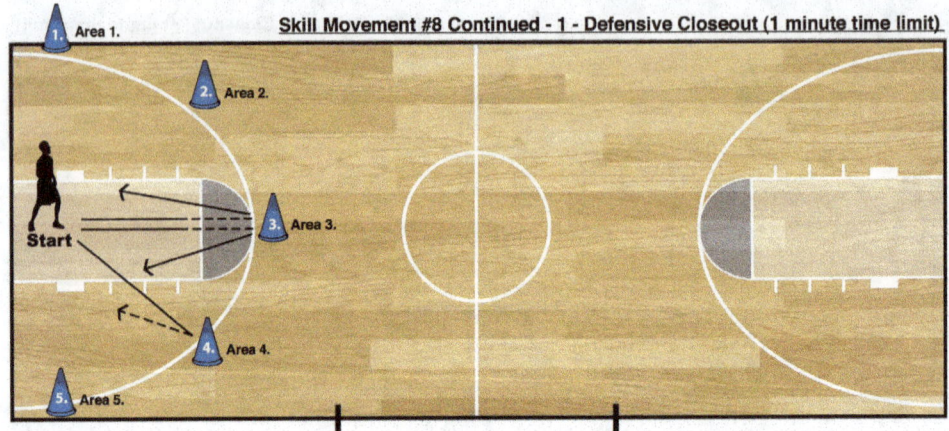

Skill Movement #8 Continued-1-Defensive Closeout (1 minute time limit)

Start out underneath the basket in the middle of the lane

3. Run out to center top of key 3 pt. line, break down in defensive stance ¾ of way with right foot in front and right hand high, stay in defensive stance and slide (go left) back towards basket to the left block
4. Run out to center top of key 3 pt. line, break down in defensive stance ¾ of way with left foot in front and left hand high, stay in defensive stance and slide (go right) back towards basket to the right block
5. Run out to right wing 3 pt. line, break down in defensive stance ¾ of way with left foot in front and left hand high, stay in defensive stance and slide (go right) back towards basket to the right block

See "Skill Movement #8 Continued-2" card

SKILLS TEST

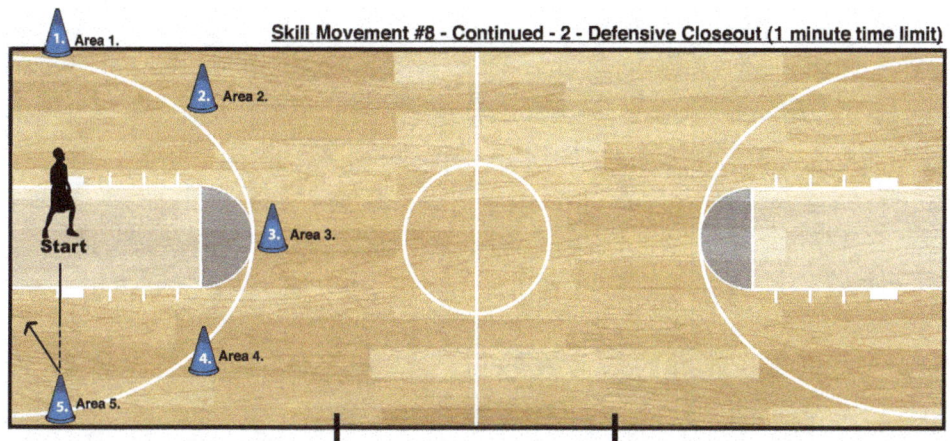

Skill Movement #8 Continued-2-Defensive Closeout (1 minute time limit)

Start out underneath the basket in the middle of the lane

6. Run out to right corner 3 pt. line, break down in defensive stance 3/4 of way with left foot in front and left hand high, stay in defensive stance and slide (go right) back towards basket between the right block and baseline

Repeat movements above continuously for 1 minute.

Results

Skill test #1 _____
Skill test #2 _____
Skill test #3 _____
Skill test #4 _____
Final Skill test _____

Chapter 2

SPOT SKILL DEVELOPMENT

Note: All warm up workouts start at the baseline. Individuals should do movements asked at the free throw line /half court line /opposite free throw line/ opposite baseline. Then repeat workout going back to your starting point.

Warm Up (Perform each movement by itself down the court and back)

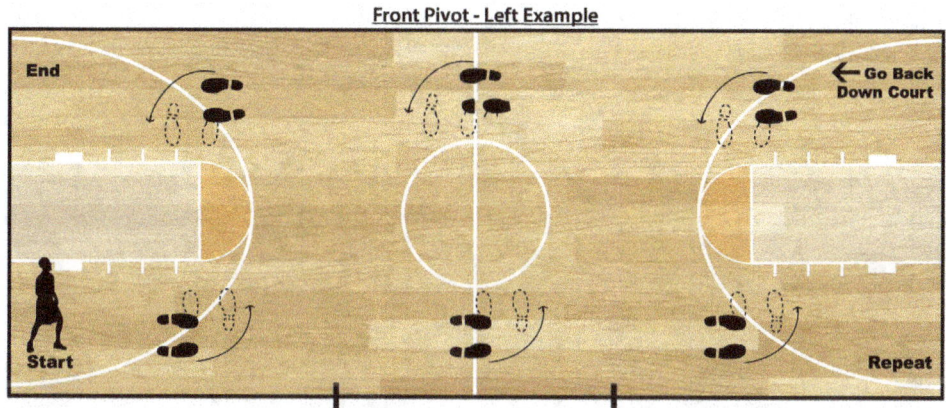

Note: All warm up workouts start at the baseline. Individuals should do movements asked at the *free throw line/half court line/ opposite free throw line/ opposite baseline*. Then repeat workout going back to your starting point.

Warm Up (perform each movement by itself down the court and back)

Jump Stop

Front Pivot Right

Front Pivot Left

Reverse Pivot Right

Reverse Pivot Left

Stutter Step

Stop and Go

Note: Perform the moves listed. Do as many repetitions as you can, then record your results after each workout. Remember to warm up and rest when needed. The B180 Basketball Fundamental Skills Program is a physically demanding workout. This is NOT for beginners or individuals with any medical condition that may be compromised by intense basketball training. Consult your physician and read the enclosed safety statement and other materials before beginning this program.

Start in the left corner behind the 3 pt. line. Locate the five (5) starting areas behind the 3 pt. line on the diagram. Go as quickly as you can to get your own rebound. In this workout always start your workout behind the three point line. Write down your results.

Follow the sequence given below.

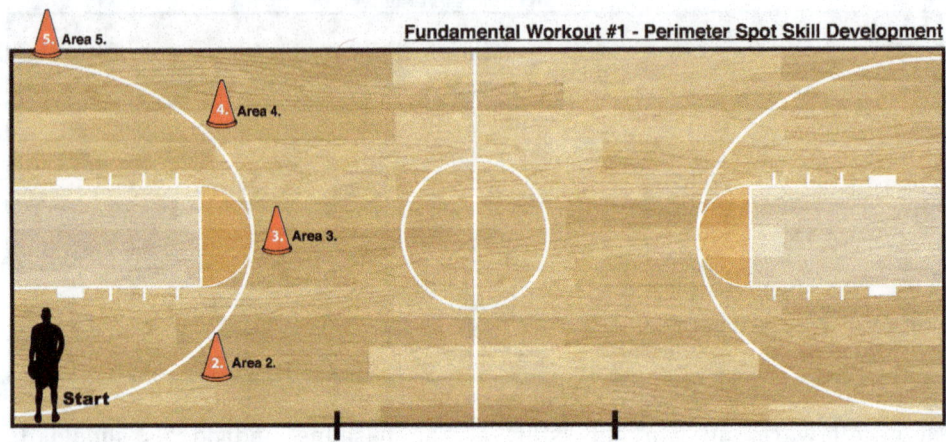

Start in the left corner behind the 3pt line. Locate the five (5) starting areas behind the 3pt line on the diagram. Go as quickly as you can to get your own rebound. In this workout always start your workout behind the three point line. Write down your results. Follow the Sequence given below.

Fundamental Workout #1-Perimeter Spot Skill Development

Start in the left corner behind the 3pt line

1. Make a 3pt shot
2. Shot fake, (go left) 1 dribble towards basket & make a pull up jump shot
3. Shot fake, (go left) 1-2 dribbles towards basket & make a left overhand layup or shot
4. Shot fake, (go right) 1 dribble towards basket & make a pull up jump shot
5. Shot fake, (go right) 1-2 dribbles towards basket & make a right overhand layup or shot

Move to next spot on diagram and repeat movements above.

Water break- 5 minutes

SPOT SKILL DEVELOPMENT

<u>Repeat workout until you make 1 shot from each task listed below</u>. Locate the starting areas on the diagram. Go as quickly as you can to get your own rebound. In this workout always start your workout (on the right block) near the basket.

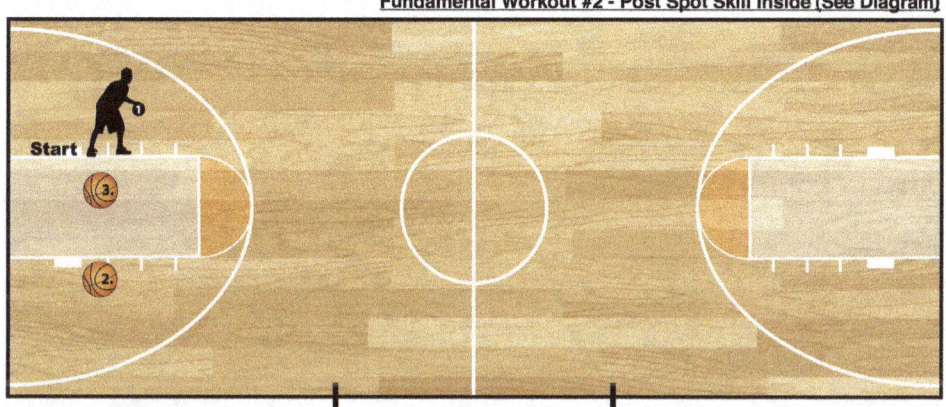

Fundamental Workout #2 - Post Spot Skill Inside (See Diagram)

<u>Repeat workout until you make 1 shot from each task listed below</u>. Locate the starting areas on the diagram. Go as quickly as you can to get your own rebound. In this workout always start your workout (on the right block) near the basket.

Follow the sequence given below.

Fundamental Workout #2-Post Spot Skill Inside (See Diagram)

Start on the right block under the basket.
1. Drop step and make a right hand layup on right block (no dribble)
2. Drop step and make a left hand layup on left block (no dribble)
3. Drop step and make a right hand jump hook in front of rim (no dribble)
4. Drop step and make a left hand jump hook in front of rim (no dribble)

Water Break- 5 minutes

B180 BASKETBALL FUNDAMENTAL SKILLS PROGRAM

Have basketballs placed at areas listed on diagram. <u>Repeat workout until you make 1 shot from each task listed below.</u> Locate the starting areas on the diagram. Go as quickly as you can to get your own rebound. In this workout always start your workout (on the right block) near the basket.

Follow the sequence given below.

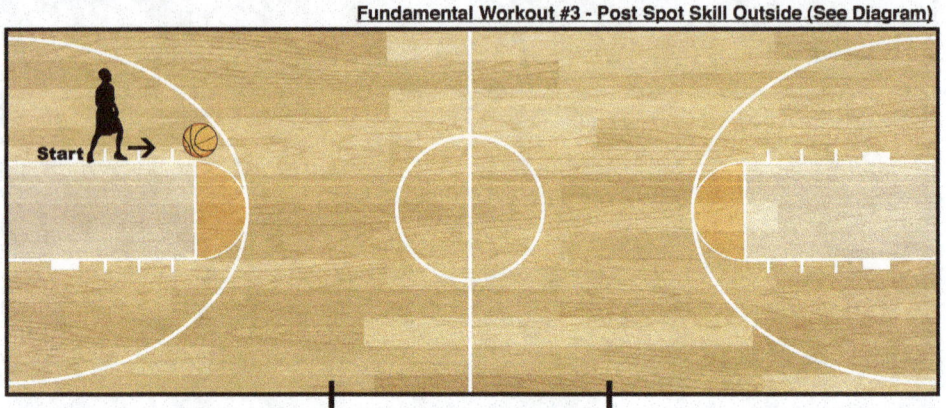

Fundamental Workout #3 - Post Spot Skill Outside (See Diagram)

Have basketballs placed at areas listed on diagram. <u>Repeat workout until you make 1 shot from each task listed below.</u> Locate the starting areas on the diagram. Go as quickly as you can to get your own rebound. In this workout always start your workout (on the right block) near the basket.

Follow the sequence given below.

Fundamental Workout #3-Post Spot Skill Outside (See Diagram)

Start on the right block under the basket.

1. Sprint to right elbow (pick up basketball) reverse pivot left and make a jump shot
2. Sprint to right elbow (pick up basketball) reverse pivot left, shot fake, 1 dribble towards basket (go left) and make a pull up jump shot
3. Sprint to right elbow (pick up basketball) reverse pivot left, shot fake, 1 dribble towards basket (go left) and make an overhand left hand shot

See "Fundamental Workout #3 Continued-Post Spot Skill Outside" card

SPOT SKILL DEVELOPMENT

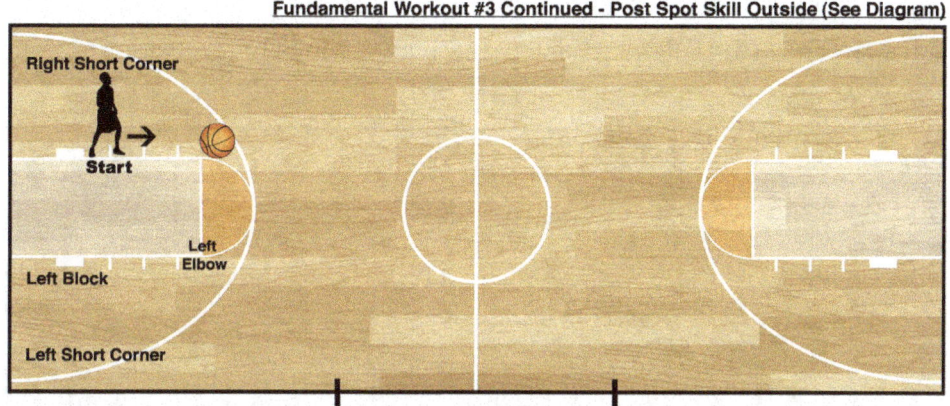

Fundamental Workout #3 Continued-Post Spot Skill Outside (See Diagram)

Start on the right block under the basket.

4. Sprint to right elbow (pick up basketball) reverse pivot right, shot fake, 1 dribble towards basket (go right) and make a pull up jump shot
5. Sprint to right elbow (pick up basketball) reverse pivot right, shot fake, 1 dribble towards basket (go right) and make an overhand right hand layup

Repeat movements above sprinting to right short corner. Go to left block and repeat movements above sprinting to left elbow and then to the left short corner.

Water Break- 5 minutes

Note: All cool down workouts start at the baseline.

Cool Down - (Run full court down and back 2 times before shooting free throws)

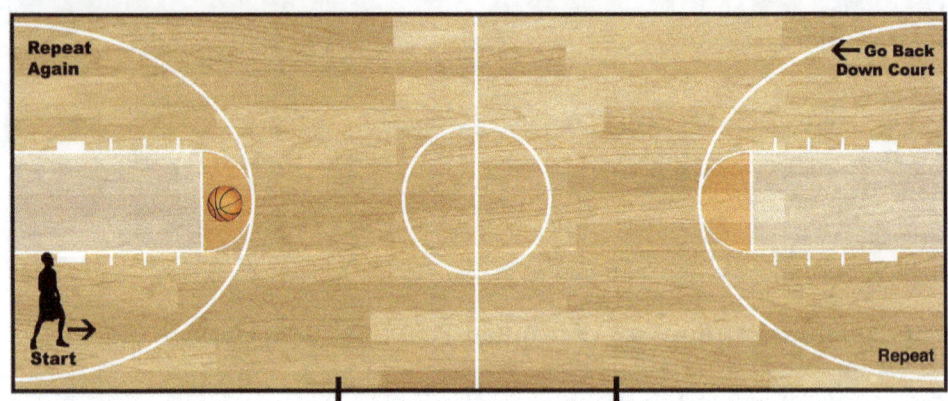

Basketball Fundamental Skills Program- Spot Skill Development

Note: All cool down workouts start at the baseline.

Cool Down-(Run full court down and back 2 times before shooting free throws)

Start on the baseline.

1. Make two (2) free throws in a row. (If you do not make the 2 free throws in a row, repeat movements in cool down listed above before trying to make 2 free throws in a row again)

Finish

Note: Perform the moves listed. Do as many repetitions as you can. Remember to warm up and rest when needed.

The B180 Basketball Fundamental Skills Program is a physically demanding workout. This is NOT for beginners or individuals with any medical condition that may be compromised by intense basketball training. Consult your physician and read the enclosed safety statement and other materials before beginning this program.

Chapter 3

B180 BASKETBALL FUNDAMENTAL SKILLS PROGRAM

Note: All warm up workouts start at the baseline. Individuals should do movements asked at the free throw line /half court line/ opposite free throw line/ opposite baseline. Then repeat workout going back to your starting point.

Warm Up (Perform each movement by itself down the court and back)

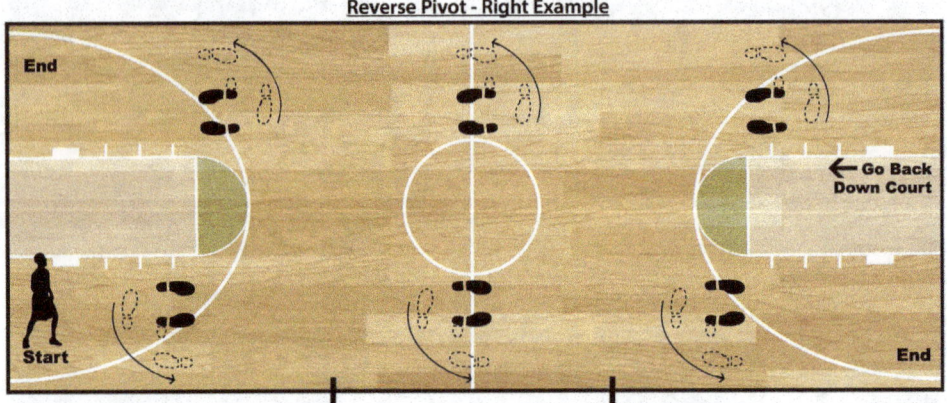

Basketball Fundamental Skills Program- Pure Shooting

Note: All warm up workouts start at the baseline. Individuals should do movements asked at the *free throw line/half court line/ opposite free throw line/ opposite baseline*. Then repeat workout going back to your starting point.

Warm Up (perform each movement by itself down the court and back)

Jump Stop
Front Pivot Right
Front Pivot Left
Reverse Pivot Right
Reverse Pivot Left
Stutter Step
Stop and Go

Note: Perform the moves listed. Do as many repetitions as you can, then record your results after each workout. Remember to warm up and rest when needed. The B180 Basketball Fundamental Skills Program is a physically demanding workout. This is NOT for beginners or individuals with any medical condition that may be compromised by intense basketball training. Consult your physician and read the enclosed safety statement and other materials before beginning this program.

PURE SHOOTING

Repeat workout until you make 11 jump shots from each task listed below before moving on to a different area. Locate the starting areas on the diagram. Go as quickly as you can to get your own rebound. No dribble is needed. The sequence should go - shoot basketball, sprint to get rebound, sprint back to area with the basketball and shoot the basketball again. Remember no dribble is needed at any point just rebound, sprint and shoot. In this workout always start your workout near the basket.

Follow sequence given below.

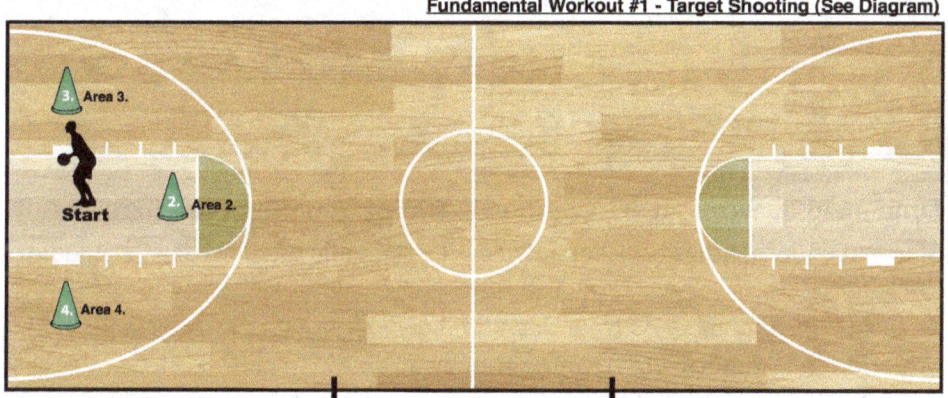

Fundamental Workout #1 - Target Shooting (See Diagram)

Basketball Fundamental Skills Program- Pure Shooting

Repeat workout until you make 11 jump shots from each task listed below before moving on to a different area. Locate the starting areas on the diagram. Go as quickly as you can to get your own rebound. No dribble is needed. The sequence should go *shoot basketball, sprint to get rebound, sprint back to area with the basketball and shoot the basketball again*. Remember no dribble is needed at any point just rebound, sprint, and shoot. In this workout always start your workout near the basket.

Follow the sequence given below.

Fundamental Workout #1-Target Shooting (See Diagram)

Start out underneath the basket between the right and left blocks in the middle of the lane.

1. Make 11 jump shots between the low post areas (shooting your normal jump shot)
2. Make 11 jump shots between the high post areas (below the left & right elbows)
3. Make 11 jump shots from the right short corner area
4. Make 11 jump shots from the left short corner area
5. Make 11 jump shots from the right elbow

See "Fundamental Workout #1 Continued-Target Shooting" card

B180 BASKETBALL FUNDAMENTAL SKILLS PROGRAM

Fundamental Workout #1 Continued-Target Shooting (See Diagram)

Start out underneath the basket between the right and left blocks in the middle of the lane.

1. Make 11 jump shots from the left elbow
2. Make 11 jump shots from the free throw line
3. Make 11 right hand layups starting from the right elbow (use 1 dribble)
4. Make 11 left hand layups starting from the left elbow (use 1 dribble)

Move to 3pt areas listed on diagram and repeat movements above.

Water break- 5 minutes

PURE SHOOTING

<u>Repeat workout until you make 3 jump shots from each task listed below</u> before moving on to a different area. Locate the starting areas on the diagram. Go as quickly as you can to get your own rebound. No dribble is needed. The sequence should go - shoot basketball, sprint to get rebound, sprint back to area with the basketball and shoot the basketball again. Remember no dribble is needed at any point just rebound, sprint and shoot. In this workout always start your workout near the basket.

Follow the sequence given below.

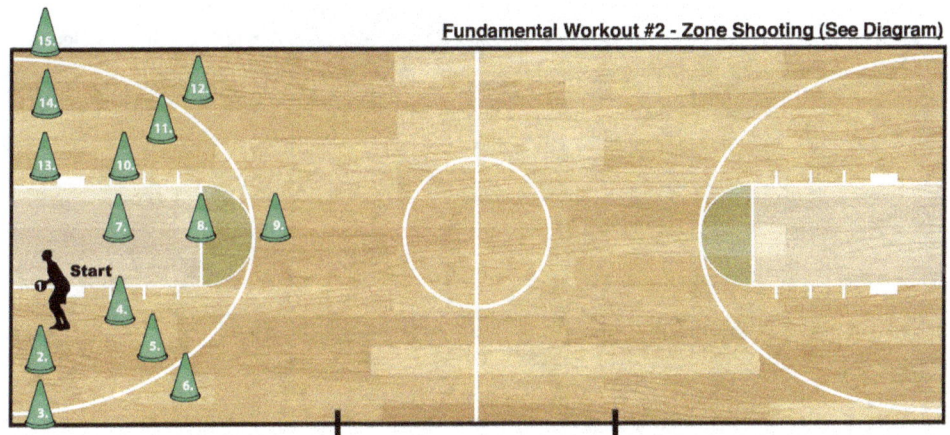

<u>Repeat workout until you make 3 jump shots from each task listed below</u> before moving on to a different area. Locate the starting areas on the diagram. Go as quickly as you can to get your own rebound. No dribble is needed. The sequence should go *shoot basketball, sprint to get rebound, sprint back to area with the basketball and shoot the basketball again.* Remember no dribble is needed at any point just rebound, sprint, and shoot. In this workout always start your workout near the basket.

Follow the sequence given below.

Fundamental Workout #2-Zone Shooting (See Diagram)

Start out near the basket on the left block

1. Make 3 jump shots from the left block
2. Make 3 jump shots from the left short corner
3. Make 3 jump shots from the left corner 3pt area

Move to next areas on the diagram and repeat movements above. Always start near the basket.

Water break- 5 minutes

B180 BASKETBALL FUNDAMENTAL SKILLS PROGRAM

<u>Repeat workout until you make 5 jump shots from each task listed below</u> before moving on to a different area. Locate the starting areas on the diagram. Go as quickly as you can to get your own rebound. No dribble is needed. The sequence should go – shoot basketball, sprint to get rebound, sprint back to area with the basketball and shoot the basketball again. Remember no dribble is needed at any point just rebound, sprint and shoot. In this workout always start your workout near the 3 pt. Line.

Follow the sequence given below.

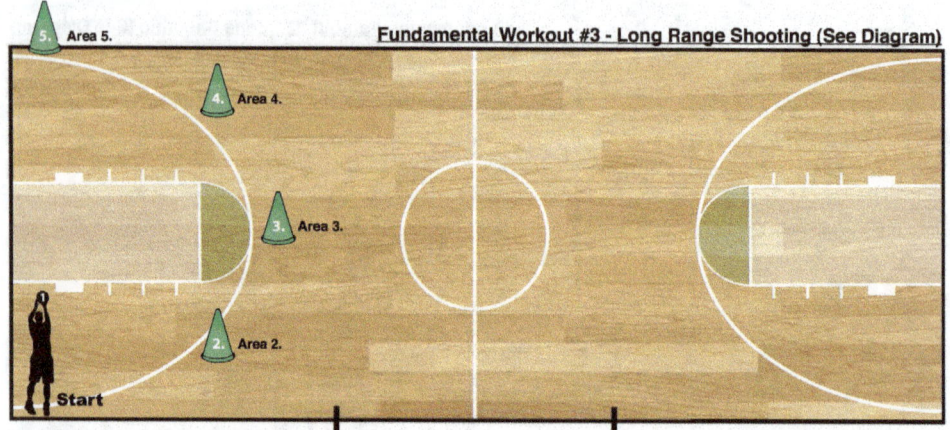

<u>Repeat workout until you make 5 jump shots from each task listed below</u> before moving on to a different area. Locate the starting areas on the diagram. Go as quickly as you can to get your own rebound. No dribble is needed. The sequence should go *shoot basketball, sprint to get rebound, sprint back to area with the basketball and shoot the basketball again.* Remember no dribble is needed at any point just rebound, sprint, and shoot. In this workout always start your workout outside the 3pt line.

Follow the sequence given below.

Fundamental Workout #3-Long Range Shooting (See Diagram)

Start outside the 3pt line in the left corner

1. Make 5 jump shots from the left 3pt corner spot
2. Make 5 jump shots from the left 3pt wing spot
3. Make 5 jump shots from the center 3pt top of key spot
4. Make 5 jump shots from the right 3pt wing spot
5. Make 5 jump shots from the right 3pt corner spot

PURE SHOOTING

Note: All cool down workouts start at the baseline.

Cool Down - (Run full court down and back 2 times before shooting free throws)

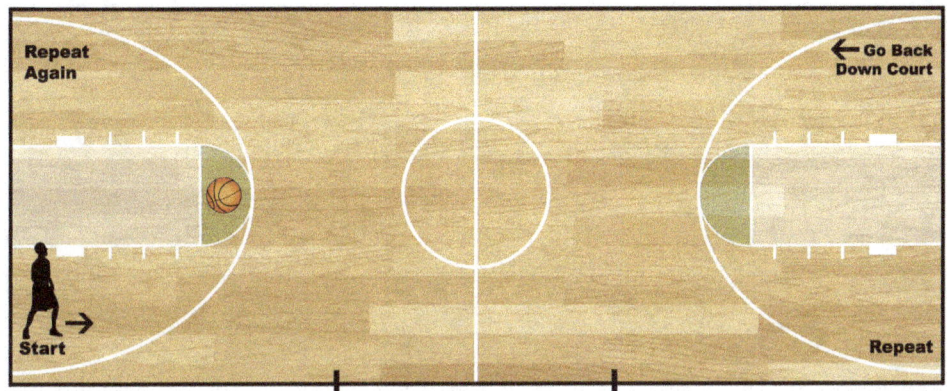

Note: All cool down workouts start at the baseline.

Cool Down-(Run full court down and back 2 times before shooting free throws)

Start on the baseline.

1. Make two (2) free throws in a row. (If you do not make the 2 free throws in a row, repeat movements in cool down listed above before trying to make 2 free throws in a row again)

Finish

Note: Perform the moves listed. Do as many repetitions as you can. Remember to warm up and rest when needed. The B180 Basketball Fundamental Skills Program is a physically demanding workout. This is NOT for beginners or individuals with any medical condition that may be compromised by intense basketball training. Consult your physician and read the enclosed safety statement and other materials before beginning this program.

Chapter 4

PERIMETER & POST FOOTWORK

Note: All warm up workouts start at the baseline. Individuals should do movements asked, at the free throw line /half court line/ opposite free throw line/ opposite baseline. Then repeat workout going back to your starting point.

Warm Up (Perform each movement by itself down the court and back)

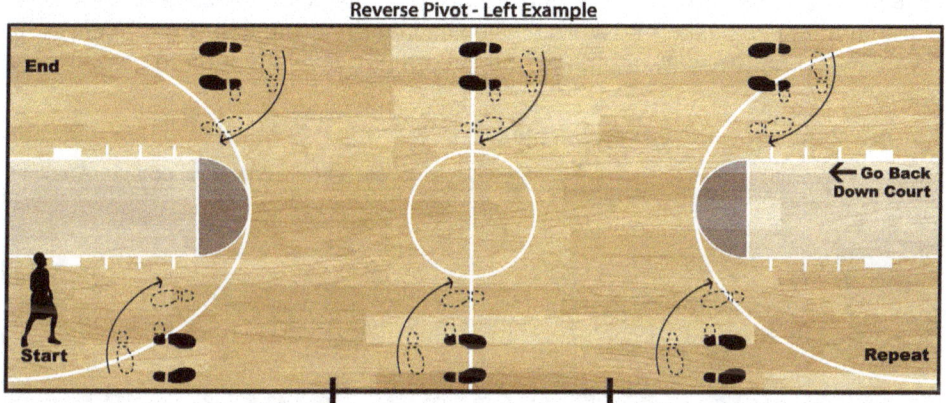

Note: All warm up workouts start at the baseline. Individuals should do movements asked at the *free throw line/half court line/ opposite free throw line/ opposite baseline*. Then repeat workout going back to your starting point.

Warm Up (perform each movement by itself down the court and back)

Jump Stop
Front Pivot Right
Front Pivot Left
Reverse Pivot Right
Reverse Pivot Left
Stutter Step
Stop and Go

Note: Perform the moves listed. Do as many repetitions as you can, then record your results after each workout. Remember to warm up and rest when needed. The B180 Basketball Fundamental Skills Program is a physically demanding workout. This is NOT for beginners or individuals with any medical condition that may be compromised by intense basketball training. Consult your physician and read the enclosed safety statement and other materials before beginning this program.

Repeat workout until you make 1 basket from each task below before moving on to a different area. Locate the starting areas on the diagram. Go as quickly as you can to get your own rebound. No dribble is needed. The sequence should go - shoot basketball, sprint to get rebound, place basketball where it should be, sprint back to starting point and repeat movements again. Remember no dribble is needed unless directed in a movement. In this workout always start your workout near the basket. Basketball is placed on the ground at the starting point if you are doing the workout alone and you do not have a person to pass you the ball.

Follow the sequence given below.

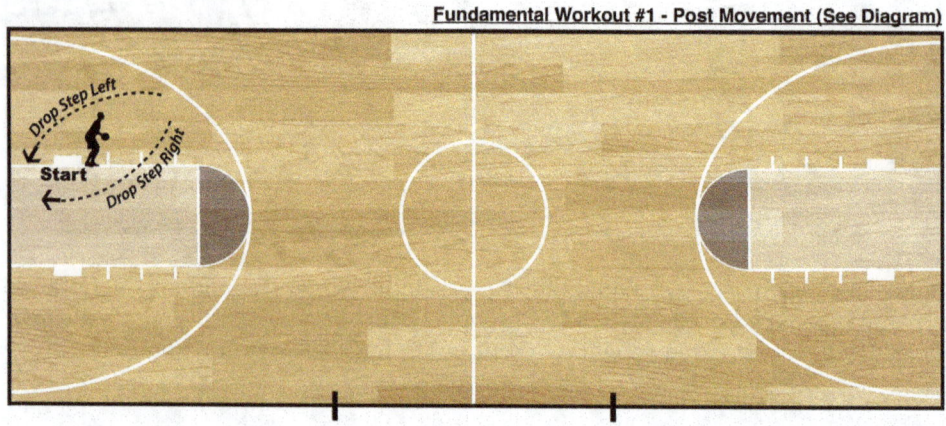

Repeat workout until you make 1 basket from each task listed below before moving on to a different area. Locate the starting areas on the diagram. Go as quickly as you can to get your own rebound. No dribble is needed. The sequence should go *shoot basketball, sprint to get rebound, place basketball where it should be, sprint back to starting point, and repeat movements again.* Remember no dribble is needed unless directed in a movement. In this workout always start your workout near the basket. Basketball is placed on the ground at the starting point if you are doing the workout alone and you do not have a person to pass you the ball.

Follow the sequence given below.

Fundamental Workout #1-Post Movement (See Diagram)

Start out underneath the basket on the right block.

1. Drop step (go left), jump stop & make a right hand overhand layup
2. Reverse pivot right, shot fake & make a jump shot
3. Reverse pivot right, shot fake, dribble and spin right & make a right hand overhand jump hook
4. Drop step (go right), jump stop & make a left hand jump hook
5. Reverse pivot left, shot fake & make a jump shot

See "Fundamental Workout #1 Continued-1-Post Movement" card

PERIMETER & POST FOOTWORK

Fundamental Workout #1 Continued -1- Post Movement (See Diagram)

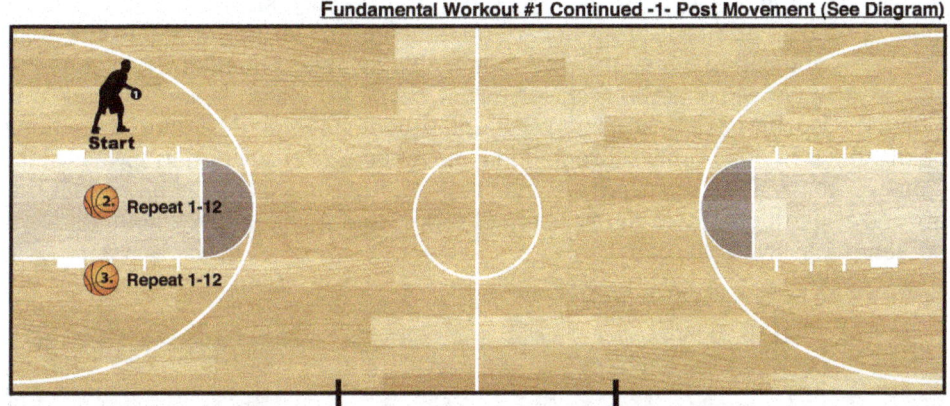

Fundamental Workout #1 Continued-1-Post Movement (See Diagram)

Start out underneath the basket on the right block.

6. Reverse pivot left, shot fake, dribble and spin left & make a left hand overhand layup
7. Front pivot left & make a fade away jump shot
8. Front pivot left, shot fake, and make a jump hook
9. Front pivot left, shot fake, spin to the right, jump stop and make a right hand over hand layup
10. Front pivot right & make a fade away jump shot
11. Front pivot right, shot fake, and make a jump hook
12. Front pivot right, shot fake, spin to the left, jump stop and make a left hand jump hook

Move to next spot on diagram (front of rim & left block) and repeat movements above.

Water break- 5 minutes

B180 BASKETBALL FUNDAMENTAL SKILLS PROGRAM

<u>Repeat workout until you make 1 basket from each task listed below</u> before moving on to a different area. Locate the starting areas on the diagram. Go as quickly as you can to get your own rebound. No dribble is needed. The sequence should go - shoot basketball, sprint to get rebound, place basketball where it should be, sprint back to starting point and repeat movements again. Remember no dribble is needed unless directed in a movement. In this workout always start your workout on the left wing behind the 3 pt. line. Basketball is placed on the ground at ending point if you are doing the workout alone and you do not have a person to pass you the ball.

Follow the sequence given below.

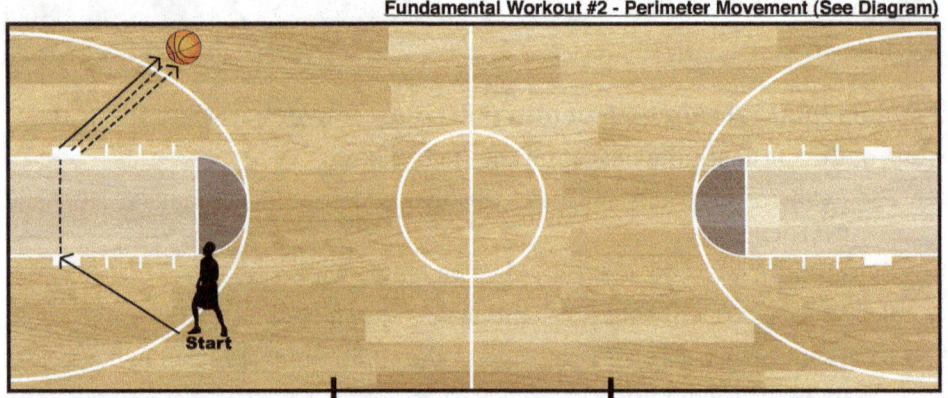

Fundamental Workout #2 - Perimeter Movement (See Diagram)

Basketball Fundamental Skills Program- Perimeter & Post Footwork

<u>Repeat workout until you make 1 basket from each task listed below</u> before moving on to a different area. Locate the starting areas on the diagram. Go as quickly as you can to get your own rebound. No dribble is needed. The sequence should go *shoot basketball, sprint to get rebound, place basketball where it should be, sprint back to starting point, and repeat movements again.* Remember no dribble is needed unless directed in a movement. In this workout always start your workout on the left wing behind the 3pt line. Basketball is placed on the ground at the ending point if you are doing the workout alone and you do not have a person to pass you the ball.

Follow the sequence given below.

Fundamental Workout #2-Perimeter Movement (See Diagram)

Start out on the left wing behind the 3pt line

1. Run to right wing (foot touches the left & right blocks), run back down and touch right block again, run back to right wing, pick up the basketball and make 1 3 pt. jump shot

PERIMETER & POST FOOTWORK

2. Run to right wing (foot touches the left & right blocks), run back down and touch right block again, run back to right wing, pick up the basketball, shot fake, (go right) 1 dribble towards the basket, and make a jump shot

See "Fundamental Workout #2 Continued-1-Perimeter Movement" card

Fundamental Workout #2 Continued-1-Perimeter Movement (See Diagram)

Start out on the left wing behind the 3pt line

3. Run to right wing (foot touches the left & right blocks), run back down and touch right block again, run back to right wing, pick up the basketball, shot fake, (go right) 1-2 dribbles, and make a right hand overhand layup

4. Run to right wing (foot touches the left & right blocks), run back down and touch right block again, run back to right wing, pick up the basketball, shot fake, (go left) 1 dribble towards the basket, and make a jump shot

5. Run to right wing (foot touches the left & right blocks), run back down and touch right block again, run back to right wing, pick up the basketball, shot fake, (go left) 1-2 dribbles, and make a left hand overhand shot

6. Run to right elbow (go down and touch the left & right blocks first), push off with inside foot at the right elbow, run out to right wing, pick up the basketball and make 1 3pt jump shot

See "Fundamental Workout #2 Continued-2-Perimeter Movement" card

PERIMETER & POST FOOTWORK

Fundamental Workout #2 Continued - 2 - Perimeter Movement (See Diagram)

Fundamental Workout #2 Continued-2-Perimeter Movement (See Diagram)

Start out on the left wing behind the 3pt line

7. Run to right elbow (go down and touch the left & right blocks first), push off with inside foot at the right elbow, run out to right wing, pick up the basketball, shot fake, (go right) 1 dribble towards the basket, and make a jump shot

8. Run to right elbow (go down and touch the left & right blocks first), push off with inside foot at the right elbow, run out to right wing, pick up the basketball, shot fake, (go right) 1-2 dribbles, and make a right hand overhand layup

9. Run to right elbow (go down and touch the left & right blocks first), push off with inside foot at the right elbow, run out to right wing, pick up the basketball, shot fake, (go left) 1 dribble towards the basket, and make a jump shot

See "Fundamental Workout #2 Continued-3-Perimeter Movement" card

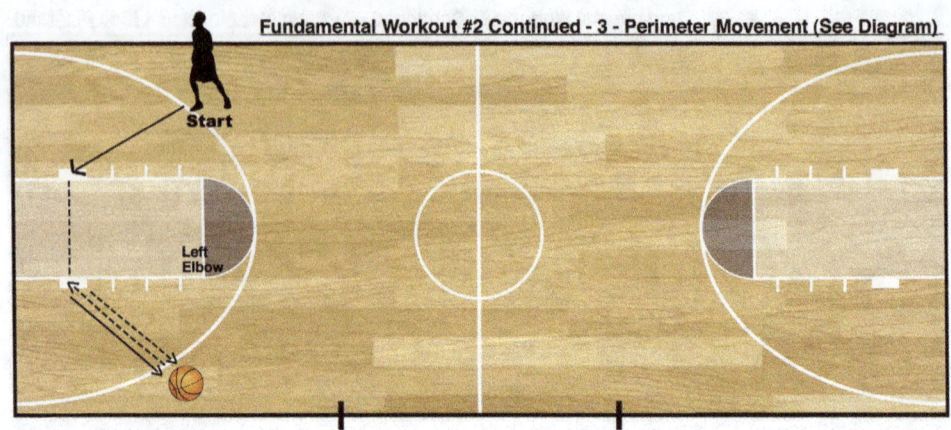

Fundamental Workout #2 Continued-3-Perimeter Movement (See Diagram)

Start out on the left wing behind the 3pt line

10. Run to right elbow (go down and touch the left & right blocks first), push off with inside foot at the right elbow, run out to right wing, pick up the basketball, shot fake, (go left) 1-2 dribbles, and make a left hand overhand shot

Move to next areas on the diagram (left wing to right wing & left wing to right elbow) and repeat movements above. Always start on wing behind the 3pt line in this workout

Water Break- 5 minutes

PERIMETER & POST FOOTWORK

Repeat workout until you make 1 jump shot from each task listed below before moving on to a different area. Locate the starting areas on the diagram. Go as quickly as you can to get your own rebound. No dribble is needed. The sequence should go - shoot basketball, sprint to get rebound, place basketball where it should be, sprint back to starting point and repeat movements again. Remember no dribble is needed at any point just rebound, sprint and shoot. In this workout always start your workout underneath the basket in the middle of the lane. Basketball is placed on the ground at ending point if you are doing the workout alone and you do not have a person to pass you the ball.

Follow the sequence given below.

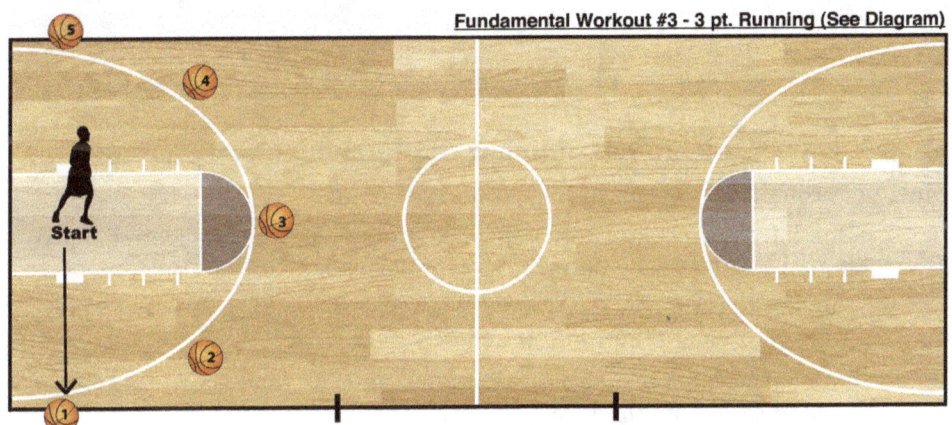

Repeat workout until you make 1 jump shot from each task listed below before moving on to a different area. Locate the starting areas on the diagram. Go as quickly as you can to get your own rebound. No dribble is needed. The sequence should go *shoot basketball, sprint to get rebound, place basketball where it should be, sprint back to starting point, and repeat movements again.* Remember no dribble is needed at any point just rebound, sprinting, and shooting. In this workout always start your workout underneath the basket in the middle of the lane. Basketball is placed on the ground at the ending point if you are doing the workout alone and you do not have a person to pass you the ball.

Follow the sequence given below.

Fundamental Workout #3- 3pt Running (See Diagram)

Start underneath the basket in the middle of the lane

1. Run out to left corner behind 3pt line, pick up the basketball and make 1 jump shot from the left 3pt corner spot
2. Run out to left wing behind 3pt line, pick up the basketball and make 1 jump shot from the left 3pt wing spot

See "Fundamental Workout #3 Continued-3pt Running" card

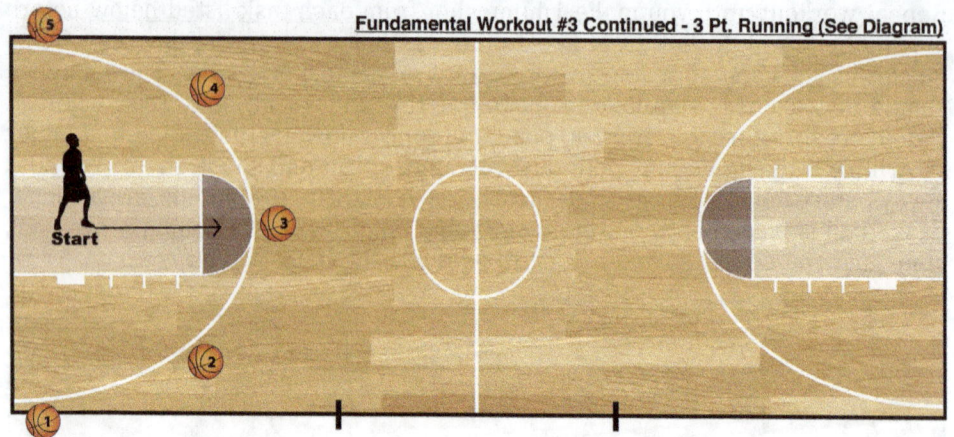

Fundamental Workout #3 Continued-3pt Running (See Diagram)

Start underneath the basket in the middle of the lane

3. Run out to the center top of key 3pt spot, pick up the basketball make 1 jump shot from the center 3pt top of key spot
4. Run out to right wing behind 3pt line, pick up the basketball and make 1 jump shot from the right 3pt wing spot
5. Run out to right corner behind 3pt line, pick up the basketball and make 1 jump shot from the right 3pt corner spot

Water break- 5 minutes

PERIMETER & POST FOOTWORK

Note: All cool down workouts start at the baseline.

Cool Down - (Run full court down and back 2 times before shooting free throws)

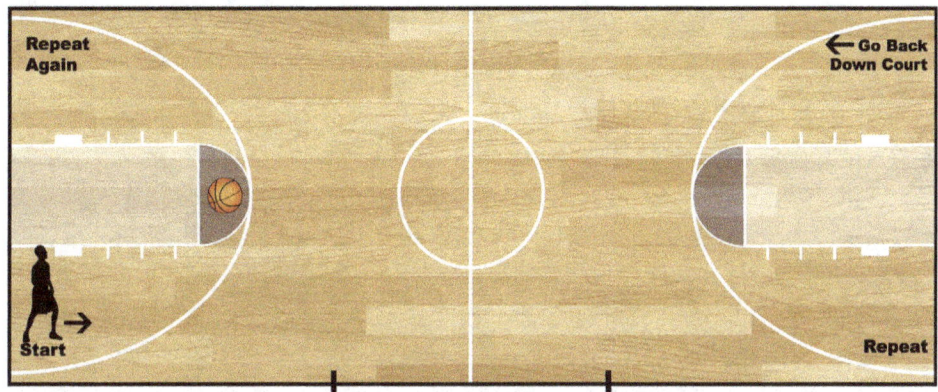

Note: All cool down workouts start at the baseline.

Cool Down-(Run full court down and back 2 times before shooting free throws)

Start on the baseline.

1. Make two (2) free throws in a row. (If you do not make the 2 free throws in a row, repeat movements in cool down listed above before trying to make 2 free throws in a row again)

Finish

Note: Perform the moves listed. Do as many repetitions as you can. Remember to warm up and rest when needed.

The B180 Basketball Fundamental Skills Program is a physically demanding workout. This is NOT for beginners or individuals with any medical condition that may be compromised by intense basketball training. Consult your physician and read the enclosed safety statement and other materials before beginning this program.

Chapter 5

DEFENSE & FREE THROWS

Note: All warm up workouts start at the baseline. Individuals should do movements asked, at the free throw line /half court line/ opposite free throw line/ opposite baseline. Then repeat workout going back to your starting point.

Warm Up (Perform each movement by itself down the court and back)

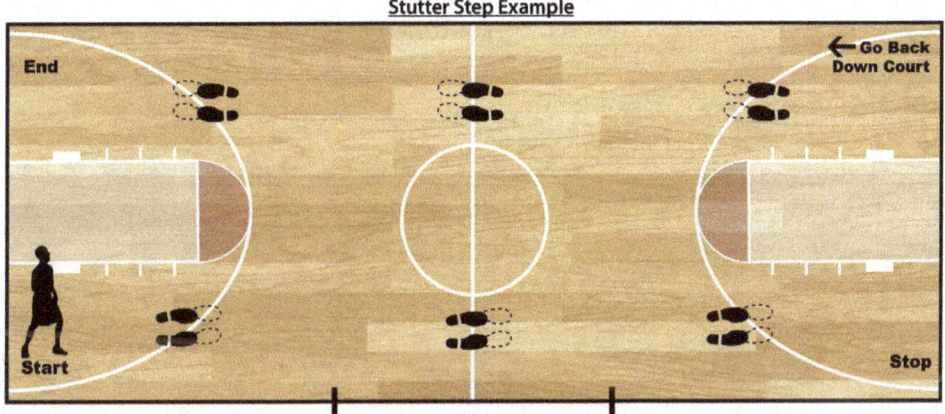

Note: All warm up workouts start at the baseline. Individuals should do movements asked at the free throw line/half court line/ opposite free throw line/ opposite baseline. Then repeat workout going back to your starting point.

Warm Up (perform each movement by itself down the court and back)
Jump Stop
Front Pivot Right
Front Pivot Left
Reverse Pivot Right
Reverse Pivot Left
Stutter Step
Stop and Go

Note: Perform the moves listed. Do as many repetitions as you can, then record your results after each workout. Remember to warm up and rest when needed.

The B180 Basketball Fundamental Skills Program is a physically demanding workout. This is NOT for beginners or individuals with any medical condition that may be compromised by intense basketball training. Consult your physician and read the enclosed safety statement and other materials before beginning this program.

Repeat workout for 1 minute. Follow the directions for each task listed below before moving on to a different area. Locate the starting area on the diagram. Go as quickly as you can to, get to the next area on the court. Place cones around the 3 pt. line in the 5 areas listed on the diagram. The movement sequence should go - run out to the cone, breakdown into defensive stance 3/4 of the way to the 3 pt. line, slide at an angle back towards the basket, go back to starting point, and repeat movements again. In this workout always start your workout near the basket in the middle of the lane.

Follow the sequence given below.

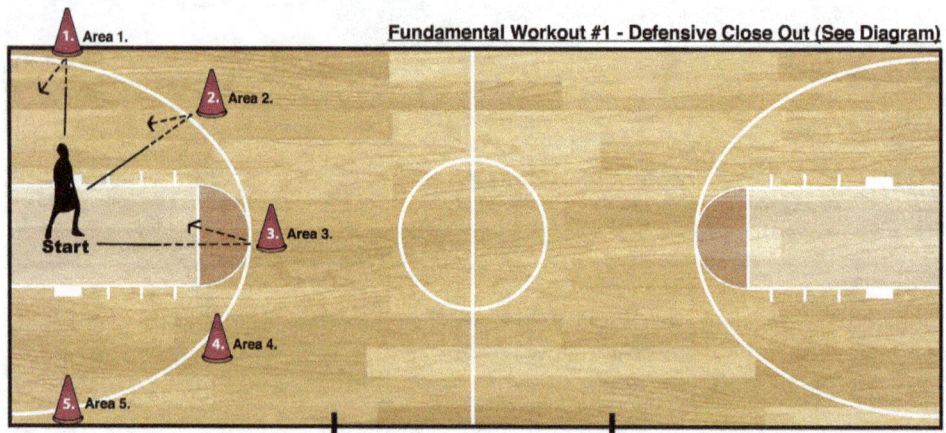

Repeat workout for 1 minute. Follow the directions for each task listed below before moving on to a different area. Locate the starting area on the diagram. Go as quickly as you can to get to the next area on the court. Place cones around the 3 pt. line in the 5 areas listed on the diagram. The movement sequence should go *run out to the cone, breakdown into defensive stance 3/4 of the way to 3 pt. line , slide at an angle back towards the basket, go back to starting point, and repeat movements again.* In this workout always start your workout near the basket in the middle of the lane.

Follow the sequence given below.

Fundamental Workout #1-Defensive Close Out (See Diagram)

Start out underneath the basket in the middle of the lane.
1. Run out to left corner 3 pt. line, break down in defensive stance 3/4 of way with right foot in front and right hand high, stay in defensive stance and slide (go left) back towards basket between the left block and baseline.
2. Run out to left wing 3 pt. line, break down in defensive stance 3/4 of way with right foot in front and right hand high, stay in defensive stance and slide (go left) back towards basket to the left block

DEFENSE & FREE THROWS

3. Run out to center top of key 3 pt. line, break down in defensive stance 3/4 of way with right foot in front and right hand high, stay in defensive stance and slide (go left) back towards basket to the left block

See "Fundamental Workout #1 Continued-Defensive Close Out" card

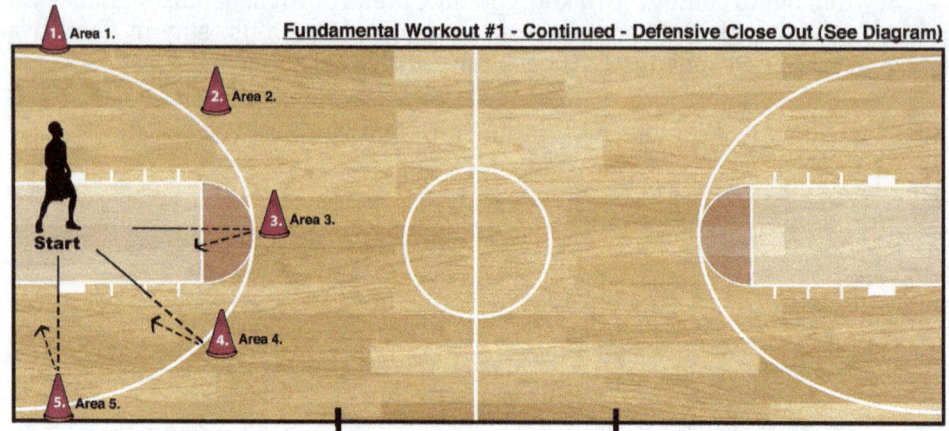

Fundamental Workout #1 Continued-Defensive Close Out (See Diagram)

Start out underneath the basket in the middle of the lane.

4. Run out to center top of key 3 pt. line, break down in defensive stance 3/4 of way with left foot in front and left hand high, stay in defensive stance and slide (go right) back towards basket to the right block
5. Run out to right wing 3 pt. line, break down in defensive stance 3/4 of way with left foot in front and left hand high, stay in defensive stance and slide (go right) back towards basket to the right block
6. Run out to right corner 3 pt. line, break down in defensive stance 3/4 of way with left foot in front and left hand high, stay in defensive stance and slide (go right) back towards basket between the right block and baseline

Repeat movements above continuously for 1 minute.

Water break- 5 minutes

DEFENSE & FREE THROWS

Repeat workout for 1 minute. Follow the directions for each task listed below before moving on to a different area. Locate the starting area on the diagram. Go as quickly as you can to get to the next area on the court. Place cones around the 3 pt. line in the 5 areas listed on the diagram. The movement sequence should go - run out to the cone, breakdown into defensive stance 3/4 of the way to the 3 pt. line, turn and box out, jump with hands high, go back to starting point and repeat movements again.

In this workout always start your workout near the basket in the middle of the lane.

Follow the sequence given below.

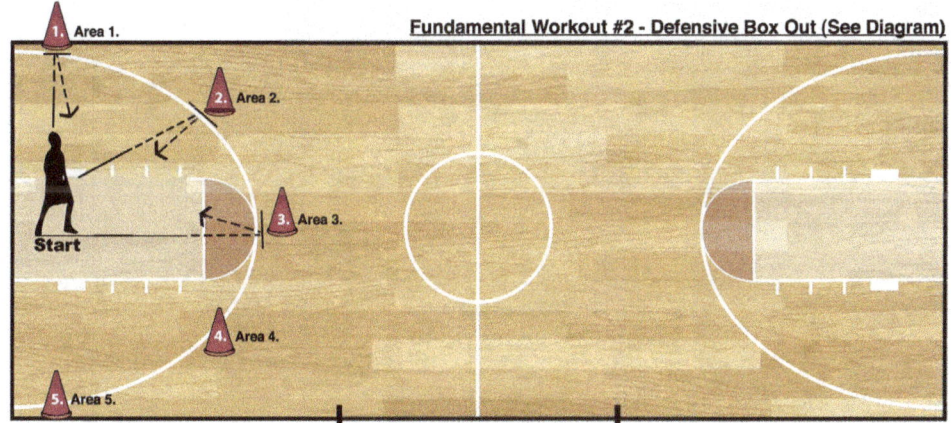

Repeat workout for 1 minute. Follow the directions for each task listed below before moving on to a different area. Locate the starting area on the diagram. Go as quickly as you can to get to the next area on the court. Place cones around the 3 pt. line in the 5 areas listed on the diagram. The movement sequence should go *run out to the cone, breakdown into defensive stance 3/4 of the way to 3 pt. line , turn and box out, jump with hands high, go back to starting point, and repeat movements again.* In this workout always start your workout near the basket in the middle of the lane.

Follow the sequence given below.

Fundamental Workout #2-Defensive Box Out (See Diagram)

Start out underneath the basket in the middle of the lane.

1. Run out to left corner 3 pt. line, break down in defensive stance 3/4 of way with right foot in front and right hand high, stay in a low defensive stance and turn to box out facing the basket. Jump with hands high. Go back to starting point

2. Run out to left wing 3 pt. line, break down in defensive stance 3/4 of way with right foot in front and right hand high, stay in a low defensive stance

and turn to box out facing the basket. Jump with hands high. Go back to starting point

3. Run out to center top of key 3 pt. line, break down in defensive stance 3/4 of way with right foot in front and right hand high, stay in a low defensive stance and turn to box out facing the basket. Jump with hands high. Go back to starting point

See "Fundamental Workout #2 Continued-Defensive Box Out" card

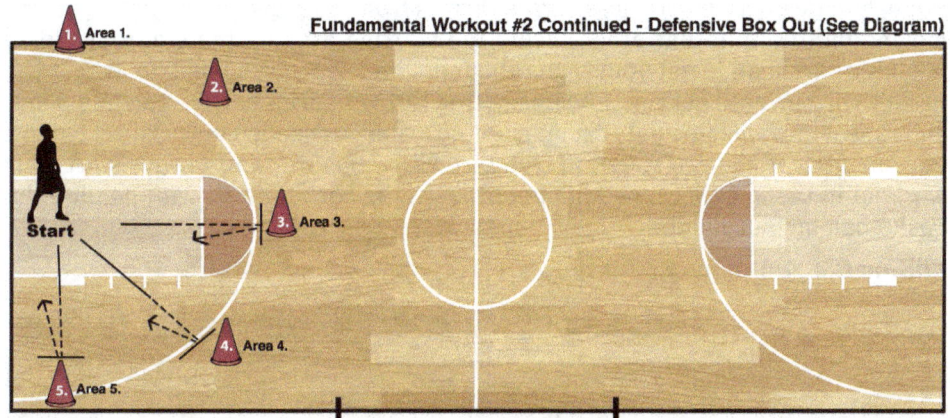

Fundamental Workout #2 Continued-Defensive Box Out (See Diagram)

Start out underneath the basket in the middle of the lane.

4. Run out to center top of key 3 pt. line, break down in defensive stance 3/4 of way with left foot in front and left hand high, stay in a low defensive stance and turn to box out facing the basket. Jump with hands high. Go back to starting point

5. Run out to right wing 3 pt. line, break down in defensive stance 3/4 of way with left foot in front and left hand high, stay in a low defensive stance and turn to box out facing the basket. Jump with hands high. Go back to starting point

6. Run out to right corner 3 pt. line, break down in defensive stance 3/4 of way with left foot in front and left hand high, stay in a low defensive stance and turn to box out facing the basket. Jump with hands high. Go back to starting point

Repeat movements above continuously for 1 minute.

Water break- 5 minutes

<u>Repeat workout until you make 5 free throws from each task listed below</u> before moving on to a different area. Locate the starting area on the diagram. Go as quickly as you can to get your own rebound. The sequence should go - shoot the basketball, sprint to get rebound, make free throws, sprint back to starting point, and repeat movements again. Remember no dribble is needed unless directed in a movement or if you are shooting free throws. In this workout always start your workout in the middle of the lane underneath the basket. Start with holding the basketball in your hand.

Follow the sequence given below.

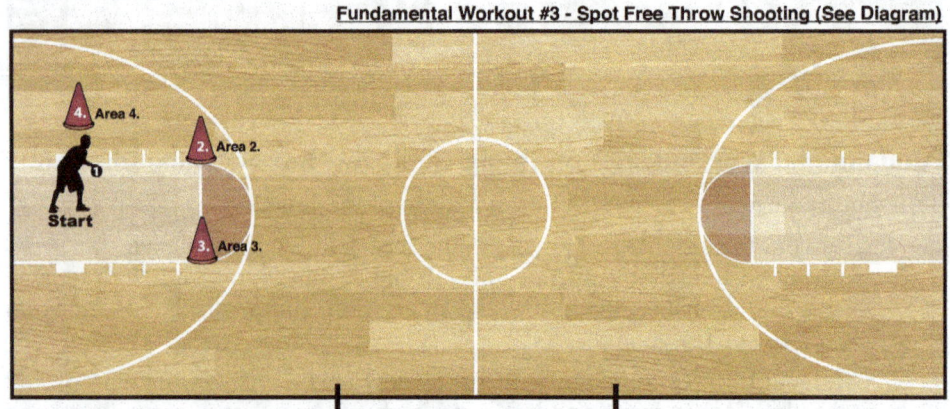

Fundamental Workout #3 - Spot Free Throw Shooting (See Diagram)

<u>Repeat workout until you make 5 free throws from each task listed below before moving on to a different area</u>. Locate the starting areas on the diagram. Go as quickly as you can to get your own rebound. The sequence should go *shoot the basketball, sprint to get rebound, make free throws, sprint back to starting point, and repeat movements again*. Remember no dribble is needed unless directed in a movement or if you are shooting free throws. In this workout always start your workout in the middle of the lane underneath the basket. Start with holding the basketball in your hand. Follow the sequence given below.

Fundamental Workout #3-Spot Free Throw Shooting (See Diagram)

Start out underneath the basket in the middle of the lane
1. Make 2 jump shots, run to free throw line and make 5 free throws
2. Run to right elbow, make 1 right hand overhand layup, make 1 jump shot, run to free throw line and make 5 free throws
3. Run to left elbow, make 1 left hand overhand layup, make 1 jump shot, run to free throw line and make 5 free throws
4. Run to right short corner, make 1 right hand overhand layup, make 1 jump shot, run to free throw line and make 5 free throws

See "Fundamental Workout #3 Continued-Spot Free Throw Shooting" card

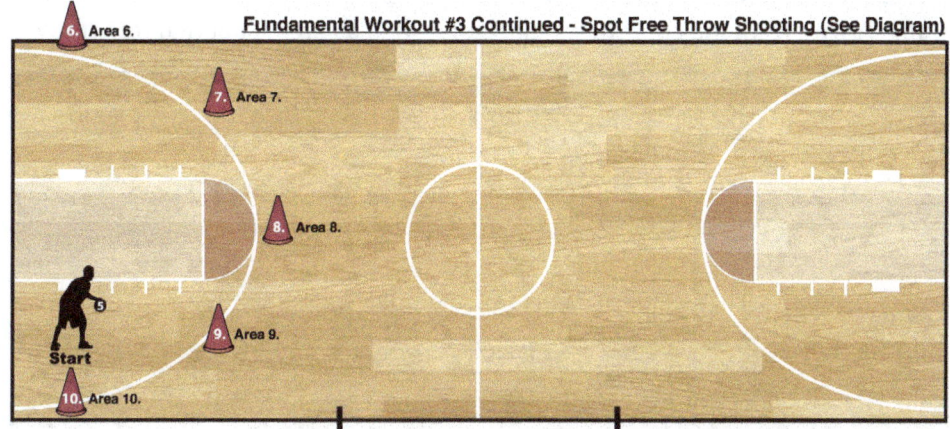

Fundamental Workout #3 Continued-Spot Free Throw Shooting (See Diagram)

Start out underneath the basket in the middle of the lane

5. Run to left short corner, make 1 left hand overhand layup, make 1 jump shot, run to free throw line and make 5 free throws
6. Run to right corner 3pt line, make 1 right hand overhand layup, make 1 jump shot, run to free throw line and make 5 free throws
7. Run to right wing 3 pt line, make 1 right hand overhand layup, make 1 jump shot, run to free throw line and make 5 free throws
8. Run to center top of key 3 pt line, make 1 right hand overhand layup, make 1 jump shot, run to free throw line and make 5 free throws
9. Run to left wing 3pt line, make 1 left hand overhand layup, make 1 jump shot, run to free throw line and make 5 free throws
10. Run to left corner 3pt line, make 1 left hand overhand layup, make 1 jump shot, run to free throw line and make 5 free throws

Note: All cool down workouts start at the baseline.
Cool Down - (Run full court down and back 2 times before shooting free throws)

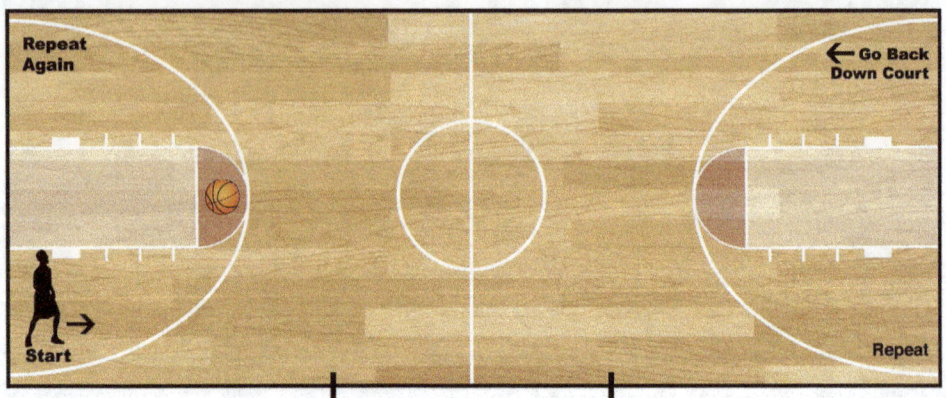

Note: All cool down workouts start at the baseline.
Cool Down-(Run full court down and back 2 times before shooting free throws)
Start on the baseline.
1. Make two (2) free throws in a row. (If you do not make the 2 free throws in a row, repeat movements in cool down listed above before trying to make 2 free throws in a row again)

Finish

Note: Perform the moves listed. Do as many repetitions as you can. Remember to warm up and rest when needed.

The B180 Basketball Fundamental Skills Program is a physically demanding workout. This is NOT for beginners or individuals with any medical condition that may be compromised by intense basketball training. Consult your physician and read the enclosed safety statement and other materials before beginning this program.

Chapter 6

Note: All warm up workouts start at the baseline. Individuals should do movements asked at the free throw line /half court line/ opposite free throw line/ opposite baseline. Then repeat workout going back to your starting point.

Warm Up (Perform each movement by itself down the court and back)

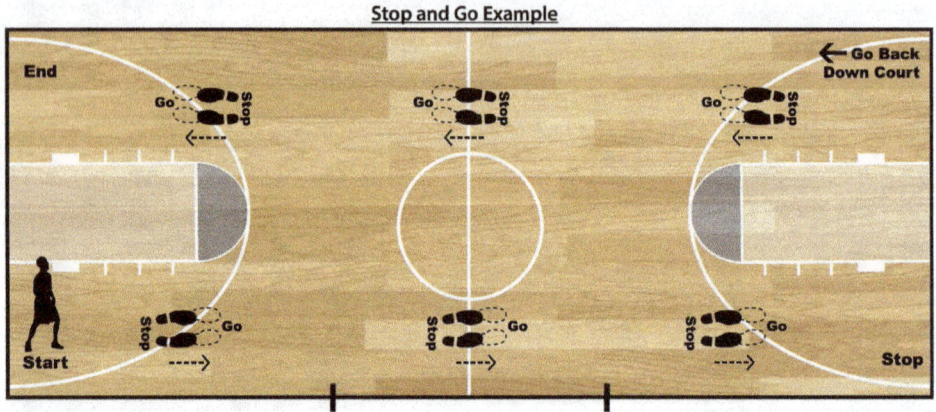

Note: All warm up workouts start at the baseline. Individuals should do movements asked at the *free throw line/half court line/ opposite free throw line/ opposite baseline.* Then repeat workout going back to your starting point.

Warm Up (perform each movement by itself down the court and back)

Jump Stop
Front Pivot Right
Front Pivot Left
Reverse Pivot Right
Reverse Pivot Left
Stutter Step
Stop and Go

Note: Perform the moves listed. Do as many repetitions as you can, then record your results after each workout. Remember to warm up and rest when needed.

The B180 Basketball Fundamental Skills Program is a physically demanding workout. This is NOT for beginners or individuals with any medical condition that may be compromised by intense basketball training. Consult your physician and read the enclosed safety statement and other materials before beginning this program.

Repeat workout for 1 minute. Follow the directions for each task listed below before moving on. Locate the starting area on the diagram. Go as quickly as you can to get to the next area on the court. Place cones at the four (4) outside 3 pt. wing areas listed on the diagram. The movement sequence should go - dribble basketball to cone, breakdown into low stance 3/4 of the way while dribbling the basketball low, slide at an angle back towards the basket, crossover and go forward, dribble to cone at the far end of the court, repeat movements again, dribble in to make a layup, go back down court repeating movements again. In this workout always start your workout on the baseline near the left corner.

Follow the sequence given below.

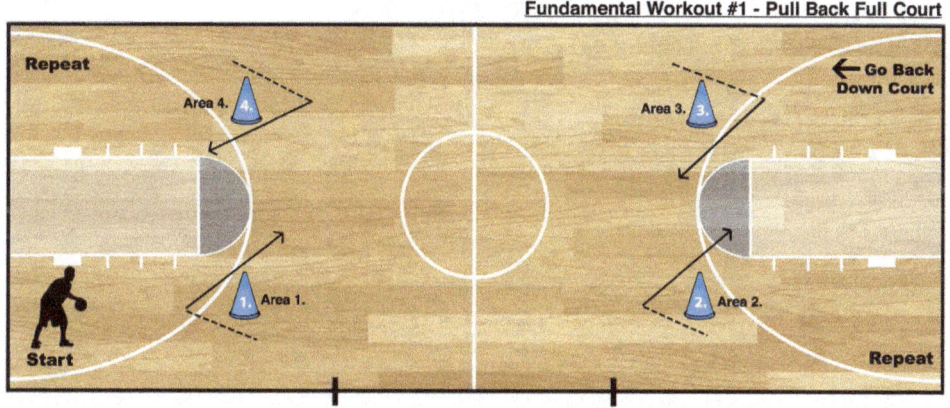

Repeat workout for 1 minute. Follow the directions for each task listed below before moving on. Locate the starting area on the diagram. Go as quickly as you can to get to the next area on the court. Place cones at the four (4) outside 3pt wing areas listed on the diagram. The movement sequence should go *dribble basketball to cone, breakdown into low stance 3/4 of the ways while dribbling the basketball low, slide at an angle back towards the basket, crossover and go forward, dribble to cone at the far end of the court, repeat movements again, dribble in to make a layup, go back down court repeating movements again.* In this workout always start your workout on the baseline near the left corner. Follow the sequence given below.

Fundamental Workout #1-Pull Back Full Court

Start on the baseline near the left corner

1. Run and dribble basketball with (right hand) to the cone, stay low and while facing forward, dribble back towards your starting point using 2 dribbles (left foot in front, eyes looking down court), crossover dribble the basketball in front of you. Then dribble forward down court in 4 dribbles.

2. Run and dribble basketball with (right hand) to the cone, stay low and while facing forward, dribble back towards your starting point using 2 dribbles (left foot in front, eyes looking down court), crossover dribble the

basketball in front of you. Then dribble forward and make 1 overhand left hand layup.

Repeat movements above continuously for 1 minute going up and down both sides of the court (start in left corner at both ends of the court)

See "Fundamental Workout #1 Continued-Pull Back Full Court" card

Fundamental Workout #1 Continued-Pull Back Full Court (See Diagram)

Start on the baseline near the left corner

3. Run and dribble basketball with (left hand) to the cone, stay low and while facing forward, dribble back towards your starting point using 2 dribbles (right foot in front, eyes looking down court), crossover dribble the basketball in front of you. Then dribble forward down court in 4 dribbles.
4. Run and dribble basketball with (left hand) to the cone, stay low and while facing forward, dribble back towards your starting point using 2 dribbles (right foot in front, eyes looking down court), crossover dribble the basketball in front of you. Then dribble forward and make 1 overhand right hand layup.

Repeat movements above continuously for 1 minute going up and down both sides of the court (start in left corner at both ends of the court)

**Repeat all movements above while starting in <u>right corner near baseline</u>. You will have 2 (1 minute) segments left. They are starting with
1. right hand dribble down and back for 1 minute-layup
2. left hand dribble down and back for 1 minute-layup

Water break- 5 minutes

Locate the starting areas on the diagram. Go as quick as you can. In this workout always start your workout on the baseline.

Follow the sequence given below.

Locate the starting areas on the diagram. Go as quick as you can. In this workout always start your workout on the baseline.

Follow the sequence given below.

Fundamental Workout #2-Walking Dribble (See Diagram) Jump Stop

Start on the baseline

1. Walk down court and dribble between the leg continuously (alternating with left & right hand). Dribble 50 times between the leg without mishandling the basketball or losing your dribble. Go down the court and back
2. Walk down court and dribble (right hand). Stay low to the ground and dribble between the legs and then crossover with your left hand in front of you. Do these movements continuously 50 times between leg and crossover without mishandling the basketball or losing your dribble. Go down the court and back
3. Walk down court and dribble (left hand). Stay low to the ground and dribble between the legs and then crossover with your right hand in front of you. Do these movements continuously 50 times between leg and crossover without mishandling the basketball or losing your dribble. Go down the court and back

See "Fundamental Workout #2 Continued-Walking Dribble" card

BALL HANDLING WISDOM

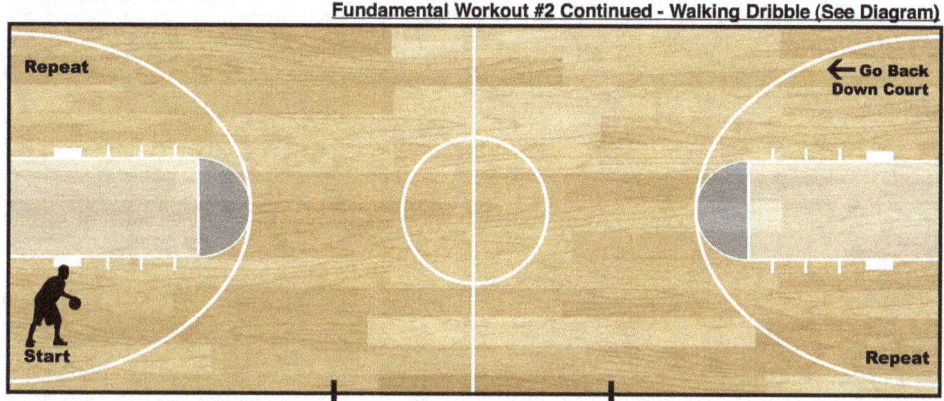

Fundamental Workout #2 Continued-Walking Dribble (See Diagram)

Start on the baseline

4. Walk down court and dribble (right hand). Stay low to the ground and dribble between the legs and then go behind your back with your left hand. Do these movements continuously 50 times between leg and behind the back without mishandling the basketball or losing your dribble. Go down the court and back

5. Walk down court and dribble (left hand). Stay low to the ground and dribble between the legs and then go behind your back with your right hand. Do these movements continuously 50 times between leg and behind the back without mishandling the basketball or losing your dribble. Go down the court and back

6. Walk down court and dribble (right hand). Stay low to the ground and dribble between the legs and then do a spin move while the ball is in our left hand. Do these movements 4 times down the court. Go down the court and back

7. Walk down court and dribble (left hand). Stay low to the ground and dribble between the legs and then do a spin move while the ball is in our right hand. Do these movements 4 times down the court. Go down the court and back

See "Fundamental Workout #2 Continued-1-Walking Dribble" card

Fundamental Workout #2 Continued-1-Walking Dribble (See Diagram)

Start on the baseline

8. Walk down court and dribble (right hand). Stay low to the ground and dribble moving the ball in and out in a circle motion (hand stays on top of the basketball). Do these movements continuously 50 times in and out without mishandling the basketball or losing your dribble. Go down the court and back

9. Walk down court and dribble (left hand). Stay low to the ground and dribble moving the ball in and out in a circle motion (hand stays on top of the basketball). Do these movements continuously 50 times in and out without mishandling the basketball or losing your dribble. Go down the court and back

10. Walk down court and dribble two (2) basketballs. Stay low to the ground and crossover dribble the basketballs in front of you. Do these movements 5 times down the court. Go down the court and back

11. Walk down court and dribble three (3) basketballs. Stay low to the ground and crossover dribble the basketballs in front of you (push 1 of the basketball slightly out in front of you while dribbling the other two). Do these movements 5 times down the court. Go down the court and back

Water break- 5 minutes

BALL HANDLING WISDOM

<u>Repeat workout until 1 shot is made from each task listed below.</u> Follow the directions for each task listed below before moving on. Locate the starting area on the diagram. Go as quickly as you can to get to the next area on the court. Place cones at the three (3) outside 3 pt. areas listed on the diagram. The movement sequence should go - dribble basketball into the lane, breakdown into low stance 3/4 of the way while dribbling the basketball low, slide at an angle back towards the 3 pt. line, crossover and go forward, dribble in to make 1 shot, go back to the 3 pt. area repeating movements again. In this workout always start your workout on the right wing behind the 3 pt. Line.

Follow the sequence given below.

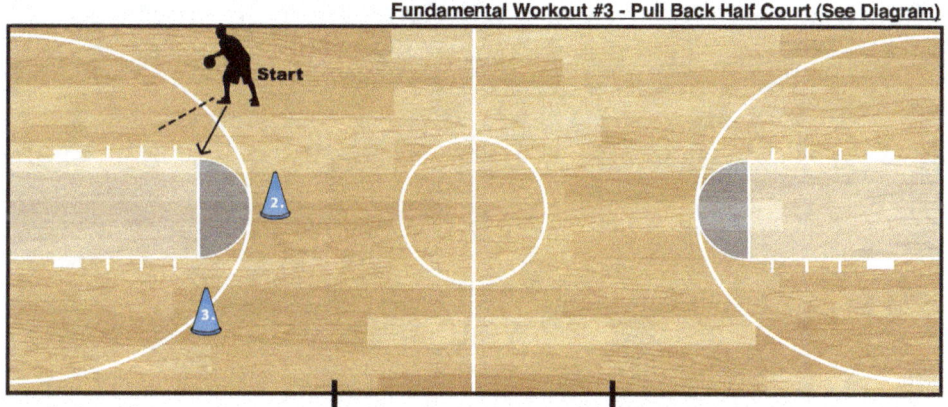

Fundamental Workout #3 - Pull Back Half Court (See Diagram)

<u>Repeat workout until 1 shot is made from each task listed below</u>. Follow the directions for each task listed below before moving on. Locate the starting area on the diagram. Go as quickly as you can to get to the next area on the court. Place cones at the three (3) outside 3pt areas listed on the diagram. The movement sequence should go *dribble basketball into the lane, breakdown into low stance 3/4 of the ways while dribbling the basketball low, slide at an angle back towards the 3pt line, crossover and go forward, dribble in to make 1 shot, go back to 3 pt. area repeating movements again* . In this workout always start your workout on the right wing behind the 3 pt. line.

Follow the sequence given below.

Fundamental Workout #3 Pull Back Half Court (See Diagram)

Start on the right wing behind the 3pt line

1. Run and dribble basketball twice with (right hand) towards the right block, make a pull up jump shot
2. Run and dribble basketball with (right hand) towards the right block, stay low and while facing forward, dribble back towards your starting point using 2 dribbles (left foot in front, eyes looking up at the basket), crossover dribble the basketball in front of you. Then dribble forward towards the lane and make 1 elbow jump shot

3. Run and dribble basketball with (right hand) towards the right block, stay low and while facing forward, dribble back towards your starting point using 2 dribbles (left foot in front, eyes looking up at the basket), crossover dribble the basketball in front of you. Then dribble forward into the lane and make 1 overhand left hand shot

See "Fundamental Workout #3 Continued-Pull Back Half Court" card

BALL HANDLING WISDOM

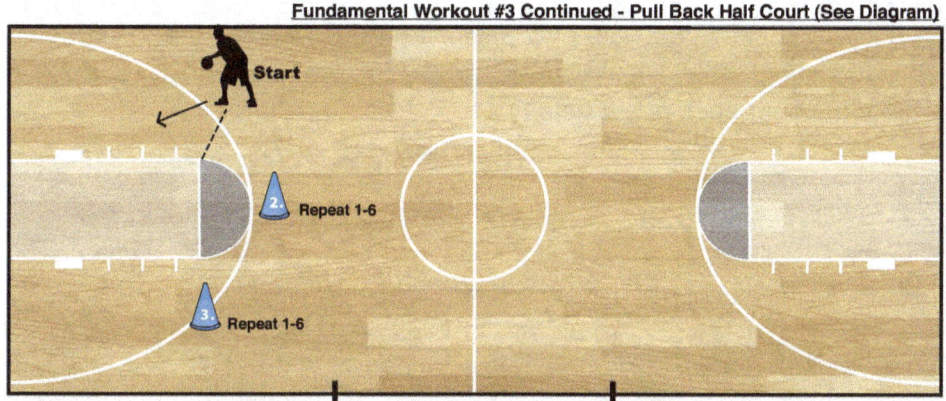

Fundamental Workout #3 Continued-Pull Back Half Court (See Diagram)

Start on the right wing behind the 3pt line

4. Run and dribble basketball twice with (left hand) towards the inside lane area, make a pull up jump shot
5. Run and dribble basketball with (left hand) towards the inside lane area, stay low and while facing forward, dribble back towards your starting point using 2 dribbles (right foot in front, eyes looking up at the basket), crossover dribble the basketball in front of you. Then dribble forward towards the right block and make 1 jump shot near the short corner
6. Run and dribble basketball with (left hand) towards the inside lane area, stay low and while facing forward, dribble back towards your starting point using 2 dribbles (right foot in front, eyes looking up at the basket), crossover dribble the basketball in front of you. Then dribble forward towards the right block and make 1 overhand right hand layup

Move to next spot on diagram and repeat movements above. The next areas would be

1. top of key behind 3pt line
2. left wing area behind 3pt line

Water break- 5 minutes

<u>Repeat workout for 1 minute</u>. Locate the starting areas on the diagram. Go as quickly as you can to get your own rebound. In this workout always start your workout on the baseline underneath the basket.

Follow the sequence given below.

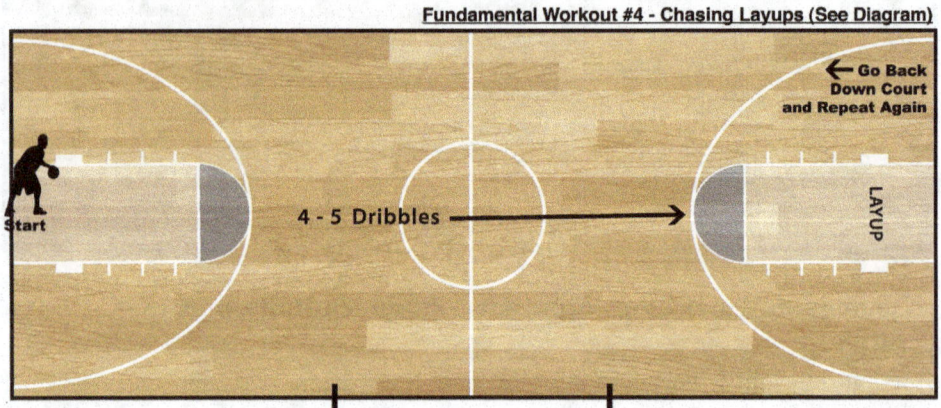

<u>Repeat workout for 1 minute</u>. Locate the starting areas on the diagram. Go as quickly as you can to get your own rebound. In this workout always start your workout on the baseline underneath the basket.

Follow the sequence given below.

Fundamental Workout #4 Chasing Layups (See Diagram)

Start on the baseline

1. Run while dribbling (alternate left & right hand) the basketball using 4-5 dribbles down court to the other basket and make a right hand overhand layup. Get your rebound
2. Run while dribbling (alternate left & right hand) the basketball using 4-5 dribbles down court to the other basket and make a right hand overhand layup. Get your rebound

Repeat movements for 1 minute

1 minute break

3. Run while dribbling (alternate left & right hand) the basketball using 4-5 dribbles down court to the other basket and make a left hand overhand layup. Get your rebound
4. Run while dribbling (alternate left & right hand) the basketball using 4-5 dribbles down court to the other basket and make a left hand overhand layup. Get your rebound

Repeat movements for 1 minute

Note: All cool down workouts start at the baseline.

Cool Down - (Run full court down and back 2 times before shooting free throws)

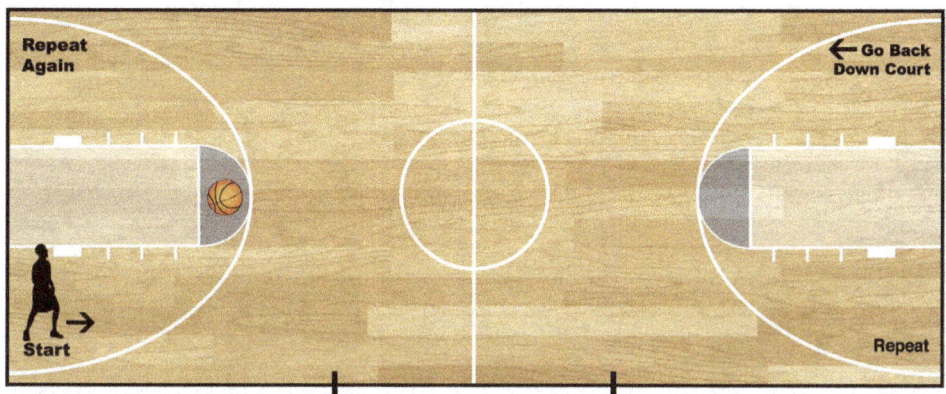

Note: All cool down workouts start at the baseline.

Cool Down-(Run full court down and back 2 times before shooting free throws) Start on the baseline.

1. Make two (2) free throws in a row. (If you do not make the 2 free throws in a row, repeat movements in cool down listed above before trying to make 2 free throws in a row again)

Finish

Note: Perform the moves listed. Do as many repetitions as you can. Remember to warm up and rest when needed.

The B180 Basketball Fundamental Skills Program is a physically demanding workout. This is NOT for beginners or individuals with any medical condition that may be compromised by intense basketball training. Consult your physician and read the enclosed safety statement and other materials before beginning this program.

Chapter 7

FOOTWORK & BALL HANDLING

Note: All warm up workouts start at the baseline. Individuals should do movements asked at the free throw line /half court line/ opposite free throw line/ opposite baseline. Then repeat workout going back to your starting point.

Warm Up (Perform each movement by itself down the court and back)

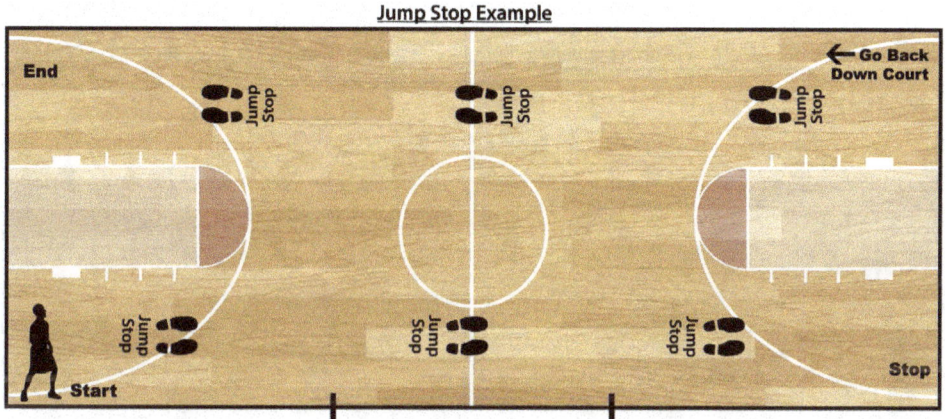

Note: All warm up workouts start at the baseline. Individuals should do movements asked at the *free throw line/half court line/ opposite free throw line/ opposite baseline*. Then repeat workout going back to your starting point.

Warm Up (perform each movement by itself down the court and back)

Jump Stop
Front Pivot Right
Front Pivot Left
Reverse Pivot Right
Reverse Pivot Left
Stutter Step
Stop and Go

Note: Perform the moves listed. Do as many repetitions as you can, then record your results after each workout. Remember to warm up and rest when needed.

The B180 Basketball Fundamental Skills Program is a physically demanding workout. This is NOT for beginners or individuals with any medical condition that may be compromised by intense basketball training. Consult your physician and read the enclosed safety statement and other materials before beginning this program.

Start in the left corner behind the 3 pt. line. Locate the five (5) starting areas behind the 3 pt. line on the diagram. Go as quickly as you can to get your own rebound. In this workout always start your workout behind the 3 pt. line. Write down your results.

Follow the sequence given below.

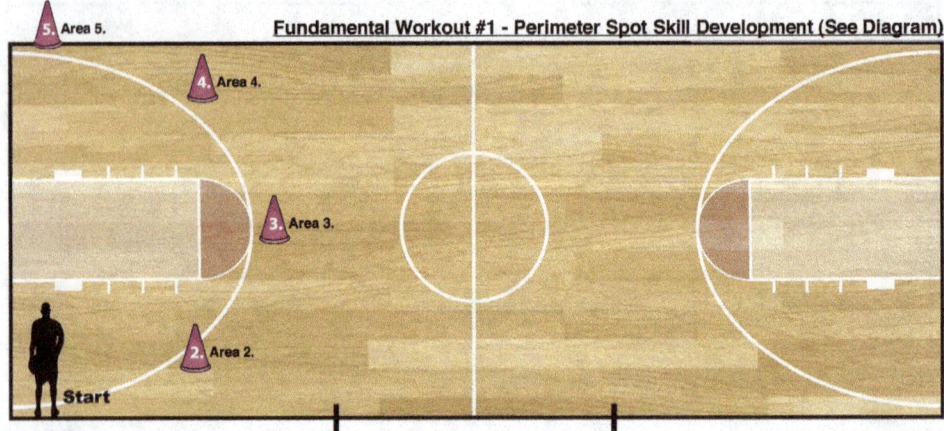

Start in the left corner behind the 3pt line. Locate the five (5) starting areas behind the 3pt line on the diagram. Go as quickly as you can to get your own rebound. In this workout always start your workout behind the three point line. Write down your results. Follow the Sequence given below.

Fundamental Workout #1-Perimeter Spot Skill Development (See Diagram)

Start in the left corner behind the 3pt line

1. Make a 3pt shot
2. Shot fake, (go left) 1 dribble towards basket & make a pull up jump shot
3. Shot fake, (go left) 1-2 dribbles towards basket & make a left overhand layup or shot
4. Shot fake, (go right) 1 dribble towards basket & make a pull up jump shot
5. Shot fake, (go right) 1-2 dribbles towards basket & make a right overhand layup or shot

Move to next spot on diagram and repeat movements above.

Water break- 5 minutes

FOOTWORK & BALL HANDLING

Locate the starting areas on the diagram. Go as quickly as you can. In this workout always start your workout on the baseline.

Follow the sequence given below.

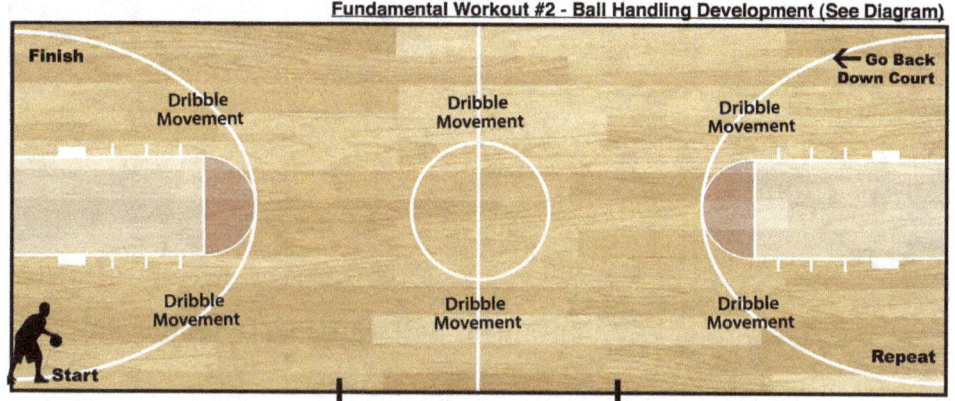

Locate the starting areas on the diagram. Go as quick as you can. In this workout always start your workout on the baseline.

Follow the sequence given below.

Fundamental Workout #2-Ball Handling Development (See Diagram)

Start on the baseline

1. Run down court and dribble (right hand) the basketball low to the ground in & out in a circle motion (hand stays on top of ball). Perform dribble movement 3 times (at free throw line/ half court/ opposite free throw line) without mishandling the basketball or losing your dribble. Go down the court and back

2. Run down court and dribble (left hand) the basketball low to the ground in & out in a circle motion (hand stays on top of ball). Perform dribble movement 3 times (at free throw line/ half court/ opposite free throw line) without mishandling the basketball or losing your dribble. Go down the court and back

3. Run down court and dribble (right hand) the basketball low to the ground stutter step as you dribble the ball down court (hand stays on top of ball). Perform dribble movement 3 times (at free throw line/ half court/ opposite free throw line) without mishandling the basketball or losing your dribble. Go down the court and back

See "Fundamental Workout #2 Continued-Ball Handling Development" card

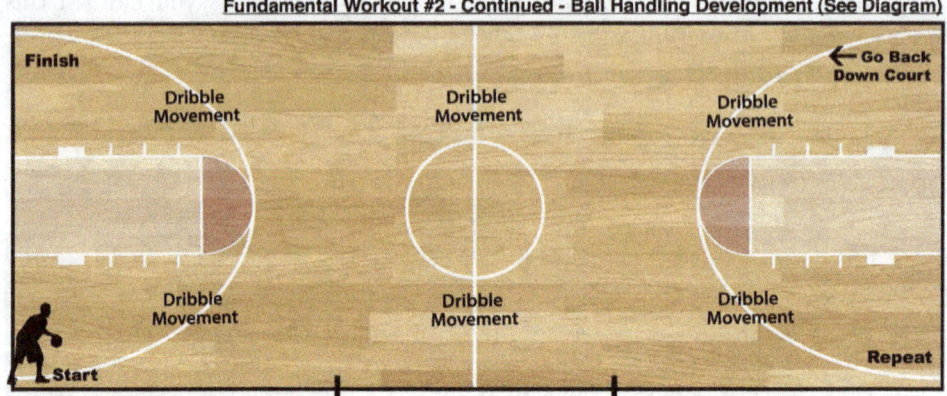

Fundamental Workout #2-Continued- Ball Handling Development (See Diagram)

Start on the baseline

4. Run down court and dribble (left hand) the basketball low to the ground <u>stutter step as you dribble the ball down court (hand stays on top of ball)</u>. Perform dribble movement 3 times (at free throw line/ half court/ opposite free throw line) without mishandling the basketball or losing your dribble. Go down the court and back

5. Run down court and dribble (right hand) the basketball low to the ground <u>cross over from right to left hand as you dribble the ball down court (hand stays on top of ball)</u>. Perform dribble movement 3 times (at free throw line/ half court/ opposite free throw line) without mishandling the basketball or losing your dribble. Go down the court and back

6. Run down court and dribble (left hand) the basketball low to the ground <u>cross over from left to right hand as you dribble the ball down court (hand stays on top of ball)</u>. Perform dribble movement 3 times (at free throw line/ half court/ opposite free throw line) without mishandling the basketball or losing your dribble. Go down the court and back

See "Fundamental Workout #2 Continued-1-Ball Handling Development" card

FOOTWORK & BALL HANDLING

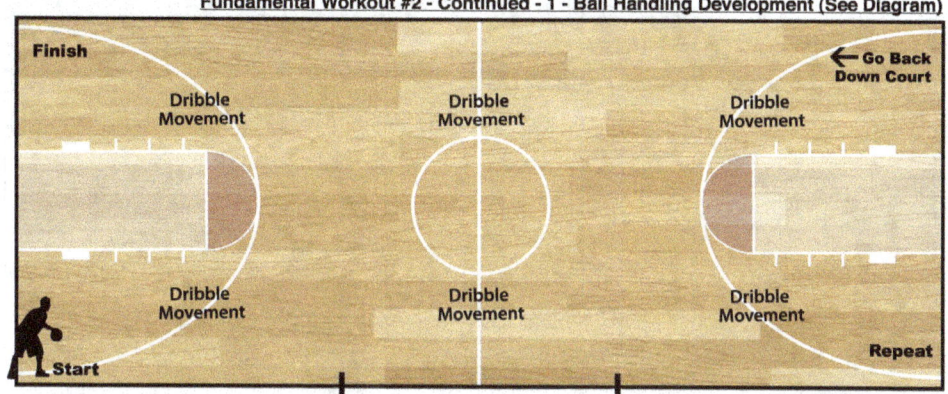

Fundamental Workout #2 Continued-1- Ball Handling Development (See Diagram)

Start on the baseline

7. Run down court and dribble (right hand) the basketball low to the ground <u>complete a full spin with the basketball going from right to left as you dribble the ball down court (hand stays on top of ball)</u>. Perform dribble movement 3 times (at free throw line/ half court/ opposite free throw line) without mishandling the basketball or losing your dribble. Go down the court and back

8. Run down court and dribble (left hand) the basketball low to the ground <u>complete a full spin with the basketball going from left to right as you dribble the ball down court (hand stays on top of ball)</u>. Perform dribble movement 3 times (at free throw line/ half court/ opposite free throw line) without mishandling the basketball or losing your dribble. Go down the court and back

9. Run down court and dribble (right hand) the basketball low to the ground <u>dribble between your legs going from right to left hand as you dribble the ball down court (hand stays on top of ball)</u>. Perform dribble movement 3 times (at free throw line/ half court/ opposite free throw line) without mishandling the basketball or losing your dribble. Go down the court and back

See "Fundamental Workout #2 Continued-2-Ball Handling Development" card

Fundamental Workout #2 - Continued - 2 - Ball Handling Development (See Diagram)

Fundamental Workout #2 Continued-2- Ball Handling Development (See Diagram)

Start on the baseline

10. Run down court and dribble (left hand) the basketball low to the ground <u>dribble between your legs going from left to right hand as you dribble the ball down court (hand stays on top of ball)</u>. Perform dribble movement 3 times (at free throw line/half court/ opposite free throw line) without mishandling the basketball or losing your dribble. Go down the court and back

11. Run down court and dribble (right hand) the basketball low to the ground <u>complete a full wrap around behind the back dribble with the basketball going from right to left hand as you dribble the ball down court</u>. Perform dribble movement 3 times (at free throw line/ half court/ opposite free throw line) without mishandling the basketball or losing your dribble. Go down the court and back

12. Run down court and dribble (left hand) the basketball low to the ground <u>complete a full wrap around behind the back dribble with the basketball going from left to right hand as you dribble the ball down court</u>. Perform dribble movement 3 times (at free throw line/ half court/ opposite free throw line) without mishandling the basketball or losing your dribble.

Go down the court and back

See "Fundamental Workout #2 Continued-3-Ball Handling Development" card

FOOTWORK & BALL HANDLING

Fundamental Workout #2 - Continued - 3 - Ball Handling Development (See Diagram)

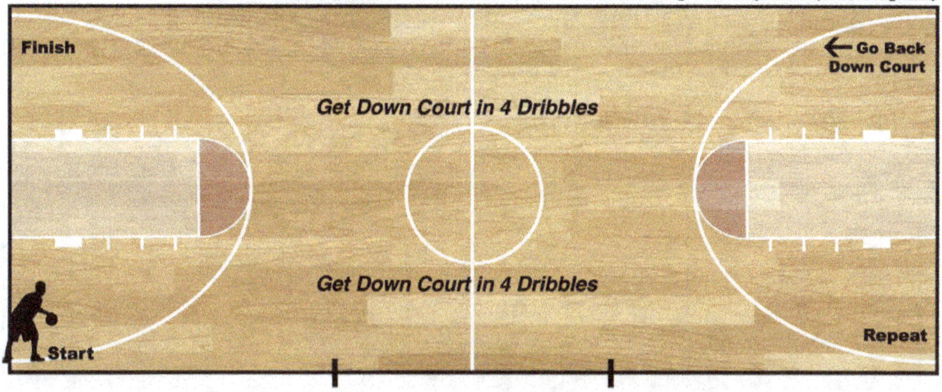

Finish
Go Back Down Court
Get Down Court in 4 Dribbles
Get Down Court in 4 Dribbles
Start
Repeat

Fundamental Workout #2 Continued-3- Ball Handling Development (See Diagram)

Start on the baseline

13. Run down court and dribble (alternate right & left hand) the basketball low to the ground <u>push dribble the ball down court out in front of you (hand stays on top of ball)</u>. Get down to the opposite baseline in 4 dribbles without mishandling the basketball or losing your dribble. Go down the court and back

Water break- 5 minutes

Stand next to a wall (a safe area) about 3-5 yards away with the basketball in your hand. <u>Repeat workout 1 time from each task listed.</u> Go as quickly as you can. In this workout always start near a wall (safe area) if you are doing this work out alone.

Follow the sequence given below.

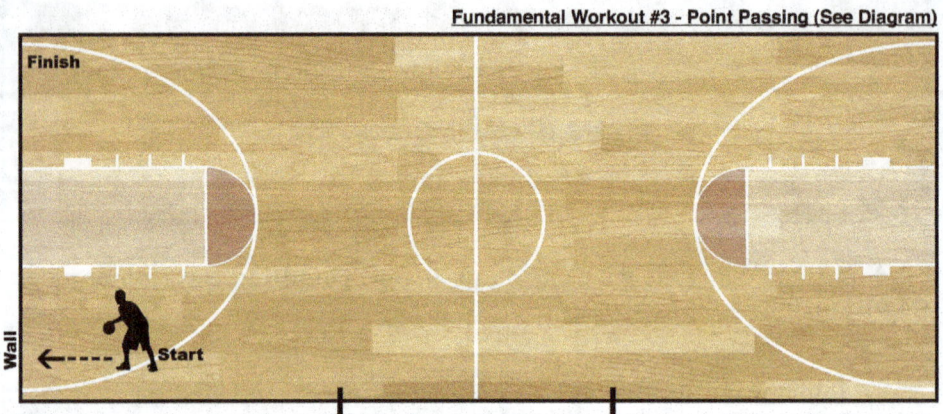

Stand next to a wall (a safe area) about 3-5 yards away with the basketball in your hand. <u>Repeat workout 1 time from each task listed below.</u> Go as quickly as you can. In this workout always start near a wall (safe area) if you are doing this workout alone.

Follow the sequence given below.

Fundamental Workout #3 Point Passing (See Diagram)

Start standing next to a wall (a safe area) about 3-5 yards away

1. Make 5 chest passes (to the same spot on the wall) and catch the basketball as it returns.

2. Make 5 right hand passes (to the same spot on the wall) and catch the basketball as it returns.

3. Make 5 left hand passes (to the same spot on the wall) and catch the basketball as it returns.

4. Bring the ball over your head and make 5 passes (to the same spot on the wall) and catch the basketball as it returns.

5. Turn to the right and make 5 behind the back passes (to the same spot on the wall) and catch the basketball as it returns.

Repeat workout until you make 25 shots from the task listed below. Start at the free throw line. Get your own rebound.

Follow the sequence given below.

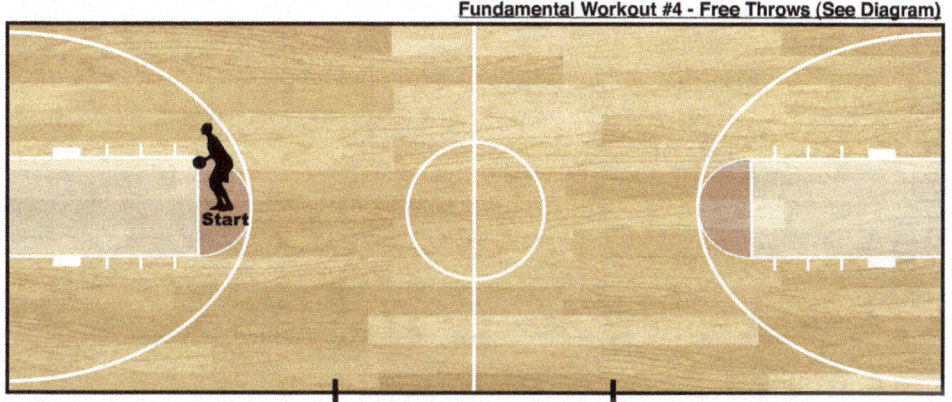

Repeat workout until you make 25 shots from the task listed below. Start at the free throw line. Get your own rebound.

Follow the directions given below.

Fundamental Workout #4 Free Throws (See Diagram)

Start at the free throw line
1. Make 25 Free Throws

Note: All cool down workouts start at the baseline.

Cool Down - (Run full court down and back 2 times before shooting free throws)

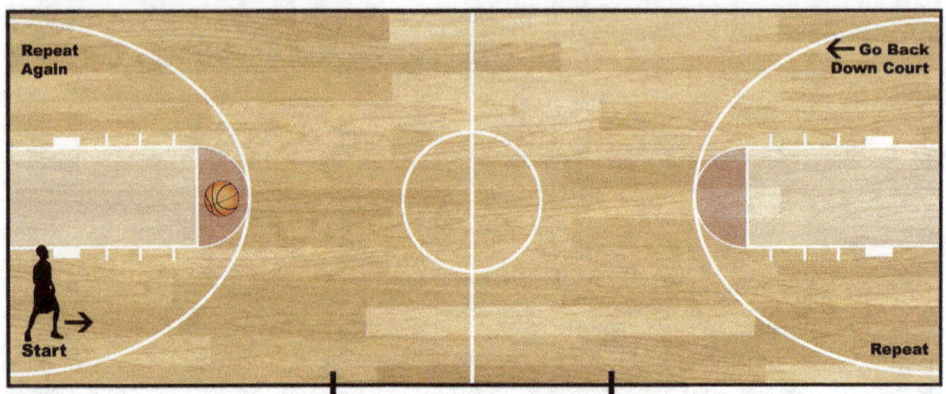

Note: All cool down workouts start at the baseline.

Cool Down-(Run full court down and back 2 times before shooting free throws)

Start on the baseline.

1. Make two (2) free throws in a row. (If you do not make the 2 free throws in a row, repeat movements in cool down listed above before trying to make 2 free throws in a row again)

Finish

Note: Perform the moves listed. Do as many repetitions as you can. Remember to warm up and rest when needed.

The B180 Basketball Fundamental Skills Program is a physically demanding workout. This is NOT for beginners or individuals with any medical condition that may be compromised by intense basketball training. Consult your physician and read the enclosed safety statement and other materials before beginning this program.

Chapter 8

B180 BASKETBALL FUNDAMENTAL SKILLS PROGRAM

Note: All warm up workouts start at the baseline. Individuals should do movements asked at the free throw line /half court line/ opposite free throw line/ opposite baseline. Then repeat workout going back to your starting point.

Warm Up (Perform each movement by itself down the court and back)

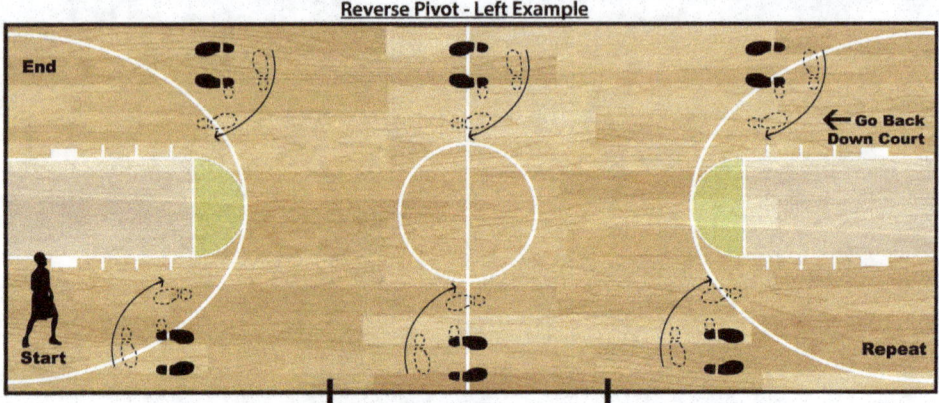

Note: All warm up workouts start at the baseline. Individuals should do movements asked at the *free throw line/half court line/ opposite free throw line/ opposite baseline.* Then repeat workout going back to your starting point.

Warm Up (perform each movement by itself down the court and back)

Jump Stop
Front Pivot Right
Front Pivot Left
Reverse Pivot Right
Reverse Pivot Left
Stutter Step
Stop and Go

Note: Perform the moves listed. Do as many repetitions as you can, then record your results after each workout. Remember to warm up and rest when needed.

The B180 Basketball Fundamental Skills Program is a physically demanding workout. This is NOT for beginners or individuals with any medical condition that may be compromised by intense basketball training. Consult your physician and read the enclosed safety statement and other materials before beginning this program.

LEVEL II SPOT SKILL DEVELOPMENT

Repeat workout until you make 3 shots in a row from each task listed below. Locate the five (5) starting areas behind the 3 pt. line on diagram. Go as quickly as you can to get your own rebound. In this workout always start your workout behind 3 pt. line.

Follow the sequence given below.

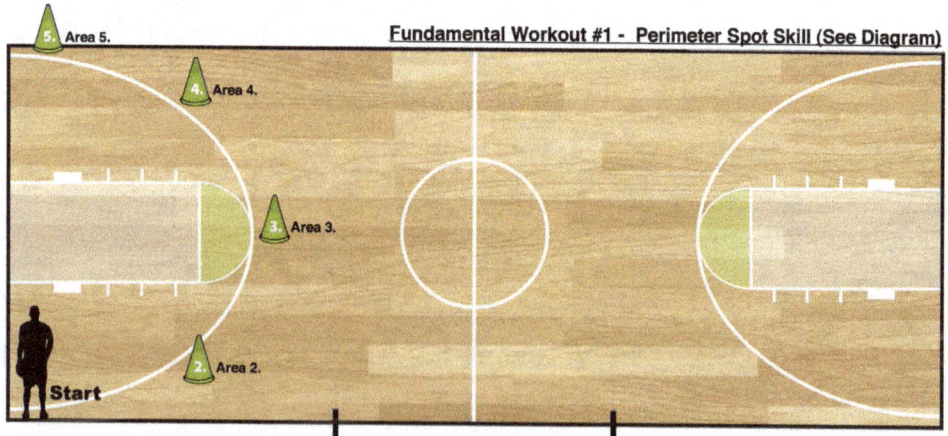

Repeat workout until you make 3 shots in a row from each task listed below. Locate the five (5) starting areas behind the 3pt line on diagram. Go as quickly as you can to get your own rebound. In this workout always start your workout behind three point line.

Follow the sequence given below.

Fundamental Workout #1-Perimeter Spot Skill II (See Diagram)

Start in the left corner behind 3pt line

1. Make a 3pt shot
2. Shot fake, (go left) 1 dribble towards basket & make a pull up jump shot
3. Shot fake, (go left) 1-2 dribbles towards basket & make an overhand layup
4. Shot fake, (go right) 1 dribble towards basket & make a pull up jump shot
5. Shot fake, (go right) 1-2 dribbles towards basket & make an overhand layup

Move to next spot on diagram and repeat movements above.

Water break- 5 minutes

Repeat workout until you make 1 shot from each task listed below. Locate the five (5) starting areas behind the 3 pt. line on diagram. Go as quickly as you can to get your own rebound. In this workout always start your workout behind the 3 pt. line.

Follow the sequence given below.

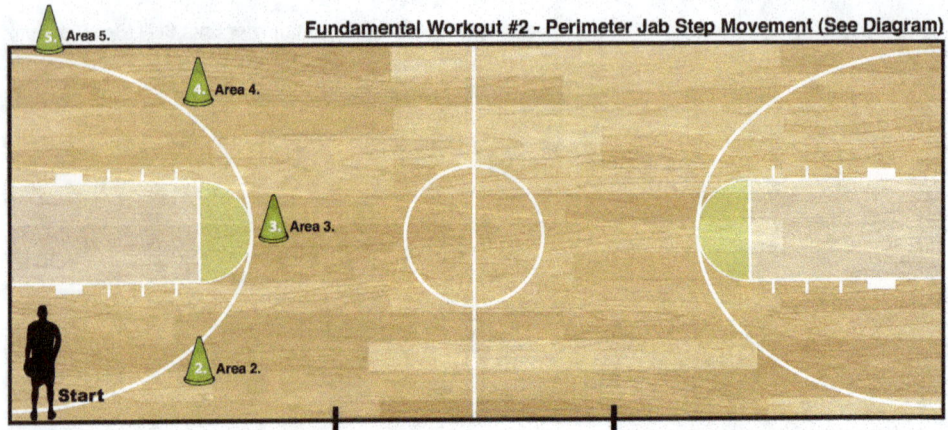

Repeat workout until you make 1 shot from each task listed below. Locate the five (5) starting areas behind the 3pt line on diagram. Go as quickly as you can to get your own rebound. In this workout always start your workout behind three point line.

Follow the sequence given below.

Fundamental Workout #2-Perimeter Jab Step Movement (See Diagram)

Start in the left corner behind 3pt line

1. Jab step (right foot) and Make a 3pt shot
2. Jab step (right foot and go right) 1 dribble towards basket & make a pull up jump shot
3. Jab step (right foot and go right) 1 dribble towards basket & make an overhand layup
4. Jab step (right foot and go left) 1 dribble towards basket & make a pull up jump shot
5. Jab step (right foot and go left) 1 dribble towards basket & make an overhand layup
6. Jab step (left foot) and Make a 3pt shot
7. Jab step (left foot and go left) 1 dribble towards basket & make a pull up jump shot
8. Jab step (left foot and go left) 1 dribble towards basket & make an overhand layup

LEVEL II SPOT SKILL DEVELOPMENT

9. Jab step (left foot and go right) 1 dribble towards basket & make a pull up jump shot
10. Jab step (left foot and go right) 1 dribble towards basket & make an overhand layup

Move to next spot on diagram and repeat movements above.

Water break- 5 minutes

Repeat workout until you make 3 shots in a row from each task listed below. Locate the starting areas on the diagram. Go as quickly as you can to get your own rebound. In this workout always start your workout (on the right block) near the basket.

Follow the sequence given below.

Fundamental Workout #3 - Post Spot Skill Inside II (See Diagram)

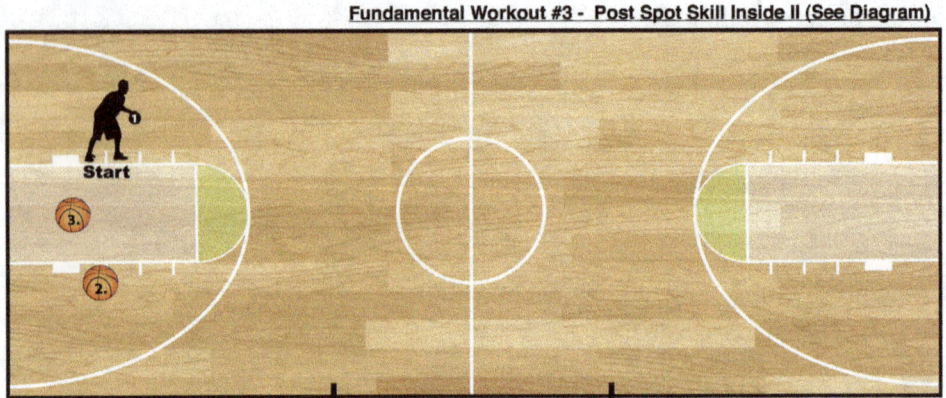

Repeat workout until you make 3 shots in a row from each task listed below. Locate the starting areas on the diagram. Go as quickly as you can to get your own rebound. In this workout always start your workout (on the right block) near the basket.

Follow the sequence given below.

Fundamental Workout #3-Post Spot Skill Inside II (See Diagram)

Start on the right block under the basket

1. drop step and make a right hand layup on right block (no dribble)
2. drop step and make a left hand layup on left block (no dribble)
3. drop step and make a right hand jump hook in front of rim (no dribble)
4. drop step and make a left hand jump hook in front of rim (no dribble)

Water break- 5 minutes

LEVEL II SPOT SKILL DEVELOPMENT

Have basketballs placed at areas listed on diagram. <u>Repeat workout until you make 3 shots in a row from each task listed below</u>. Locate the starting areas on the diagram. Go as quickly as you can to get your own rebound. In this workout always start your workout (on the right block) near the basket.

Follow the sequence given below.

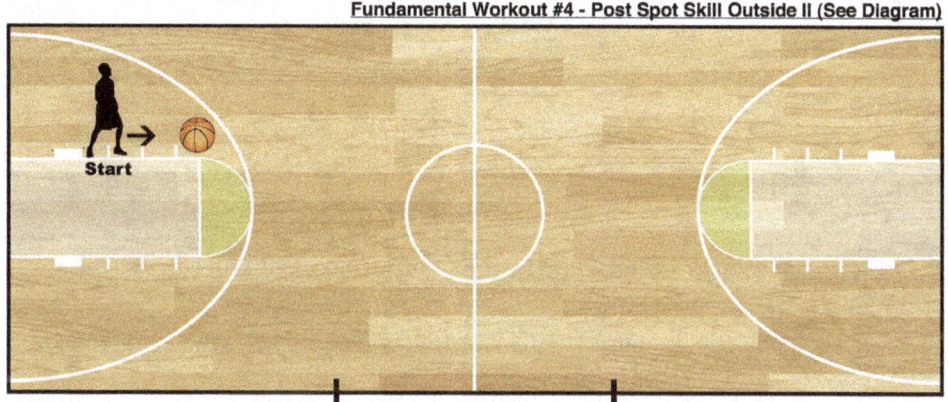

Fundamental Workout #4 - Post Spot Skill Outside II (See Diagram)

Have basketballs placed at areas listed on diagram. <u>Repeat workout until you make 3 shots in a row from each task listed below</u>. Locate the starting areas on the diagram. Go as quickly as you can to get your own rebound. In this workout always start your workout (on the right block) near the basket.

Follow the sequence given below.

Fundamental Workout #4-Post Spot Skill Outside II (See Diagram)

Start on the right block under the basket

1. Sprint to right elbow (pick up basketball) reverse pivot left and make a jump shot
2. Sprint to right elbow (pick up basketball) reverse pivot left, shot fake, 1 dribble towards basket (go left) and make a pull up jump shot
3. Sprint to right elbow (pick up basketball) reverse pivot left, shot fake, 1 dribble towards basket (go left) and make an overhand left hand shot

See "Fundamental Workout #4 Continued-Post Spot Skill Outside II" card

Fundamental Workout #4 - Continued Post Spot Skill Outside II (See Diagram)

Start on the right block under the basket-(make 3 shots in a row from each task listed below)

4. Sprint to right elbow (pick up basketball) reverse pivot right, shot fake, 1 dribble towards basket (go right) and make a pull up jump shot
5. Sprint to right elbow (pick up basketball) reverse pivot right, shot fake, 1 dribble towards basket (go right) and make an overhand right hand layup

Repeat movements above sprinting to right short corner. Go to left block and repeat movements above sprinting to left elbow and then to the left short corner.

Water break- 5 minutes

LEVEL II SPOT SKILL DEVELOPMENT

Have basketballs placed at areas listed on diagram. <u>Repeat workout until you make 1 shot in a row from each task listed below.</u> Locate the starting areas on the diagram. Go as quickly as you can to get your own rebound. In this workout always start your workout (on the right block) near the basket.

Follow the sequence given below.

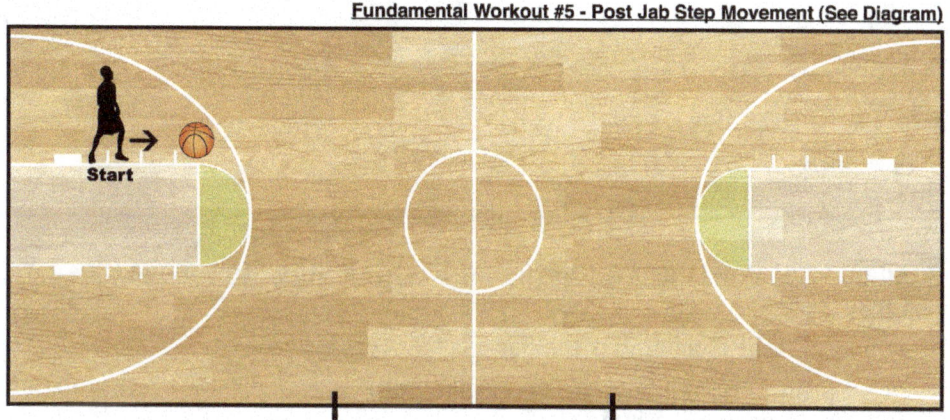

Have basketballs placed at areas listed on diagram. <u>Repeat workout until you make 1 shot from each task listed below</u>. Locate the starting areas on the diagram. Go as quickly as you can to get your own rebound. In this workout always start your workout (on the right block) near the basket.

Follow the sequence given below.

Fundamental Workout #5-Post Jab Step Movement (See Diagram)

Start on the right block under the basket

1. Sprint to right elbow (pick up basketball) reverse pivot left, *jab step (right foot)* and make a jump shot
2. Sprint to right elbow (pick up basketball) reverse pivot left, *jab step (right foot)*, 1 dribble towards basket (go left) and make a pull up jump shot
3. Sprint to right elbow (pick up basketball) reverse pivot left, *jab step (right foot)*, 1 dribble towards basket (go left) and make an overhand left hand shot

See "Fundamental Workout #5 Continued-Post Jab Step Movement" card

Fundamental Workout #5-Continued-Post Jab Step Movement (See Diagram)

Start on the right block under the basket

4. Sprint to right elbow (pick up basketball) reverse pivot left, jab step (left foot) and make a jump shot
5. Sprint to right elbow (pick up basketball) reverse pivot right, jab step (left foot), 1 dribble towards basket (go right) and make a pull up jump shot
6. Sprint to right elbow (pick up basketball) reverse pivot right, jab step (left foot), 1 dribble towards basket (go right) and make an overhand right hand layup

Repeat movements above sprinting to right short corner. Go to left block and repeat movements above sprinting to left elbow and then to the left short corner.

Water break- 5 minutes

LEVEL II SPOT SKILL DEVELOPMENT

Note: All cool down workouts start at the baseline.

Cool Down - (Run full court down and back 2 times before shooting free throws)

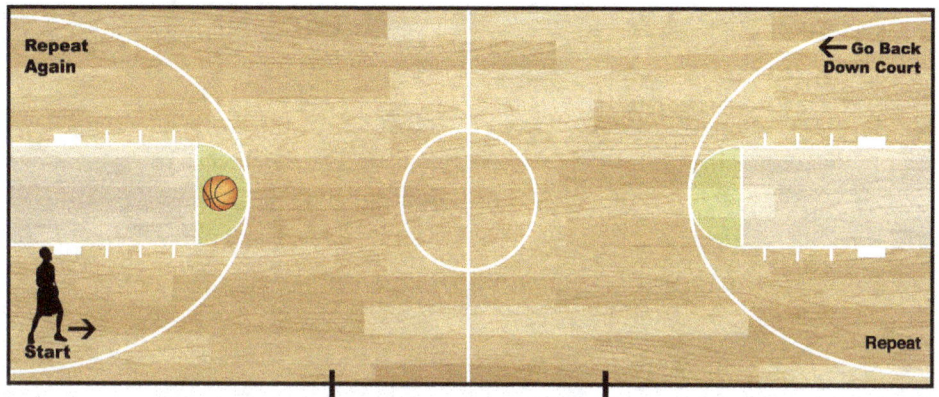

Note: All cool down workouts start at the baseline.

Cool Down-(Run full court down and back 2 times before shooting free throws)

Start on the baseline.

1. Make two (2) free throws in a row. (If you do not make the 2 free throws in a row, repeat movements in cool down listed above before trying to make 2 free throws in a row again)

Finish

Note: Perform the moves listed. Do as many repetitions as you can. Remember to warm up and rest when needed.

The B180 Basketball Fundamental Skills Program is a physically demanding workout. This is NOT for beginners or individuals with any medical condition that may be compromised by intense basketball training. Consult your physician and read the enclosed safety statement and other materials before beginning this program.

Chapter 9

LEVEL II PERIMETER & POST FOOTWORK

Note: All warm up workouts start at the baseline. Individuals should do movements asked at the free throw line /half court line/ opposite free throw line/ opposite baseline. Then repeat workout going back to your starting point.

Warm Up (Perform each movement by itself down the court and back)

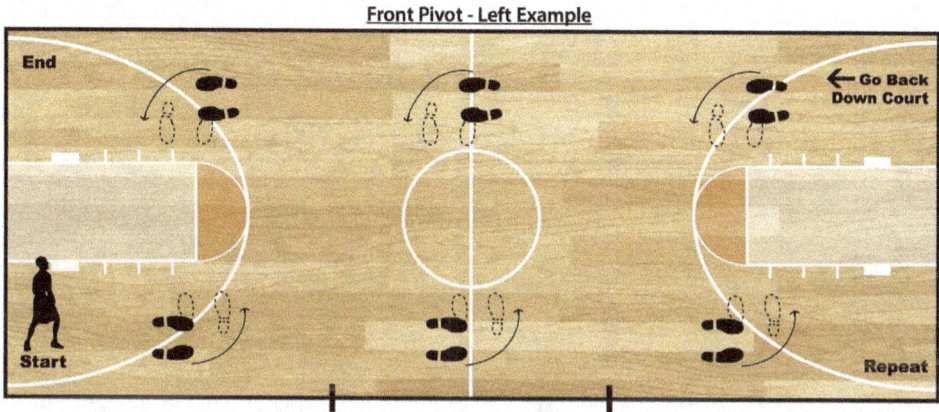

Front Pivot - Left Example

Note: All warm up workouts start at the baseline. Individuals should do movements asked at the free throw line/half court line/ opposite free throw line/ opposite baseline. Then repeat workout going back to your starting point.

Warm Up (perform each movement by itself down the court and back)

Jump Stop
Front Pivot Right
Front Pivot Left
Reverse Pivot Right
Reverse Pivot Left
Stutter Step
Stop and Go

Note: Perform the moves listed. Do as many repetitions as you can, then record your results after each workout. Remember to warm up and rest when needed.

The B180 Basketball Fundamental Skills Program is a physically demanding workout. This is NOT for beginners or individuals with any medical condition that may be compromised by intense basketball training. Consult your physician and read the enclosed safety statement and other materials before beginning this program.

Repeat workout until you make 5 baskets from each task listed below before moving on to a different area. Locate the starting areas on the diagram. Go as quickly as you can to get your own rebound. No dribble is needed. The sequence should go - shoot basketball, sprint to get rebound, place basketball where it should be, sprint back to starting point and repeat movements again. Remember no dribble is needed unless directed in a movement. In this workout always start your workout near the basket. Basketball is placed on the ground at the starting point if you are doing the workout alone and you do not have a person to pass you the ball.

Follow the sequence given below.

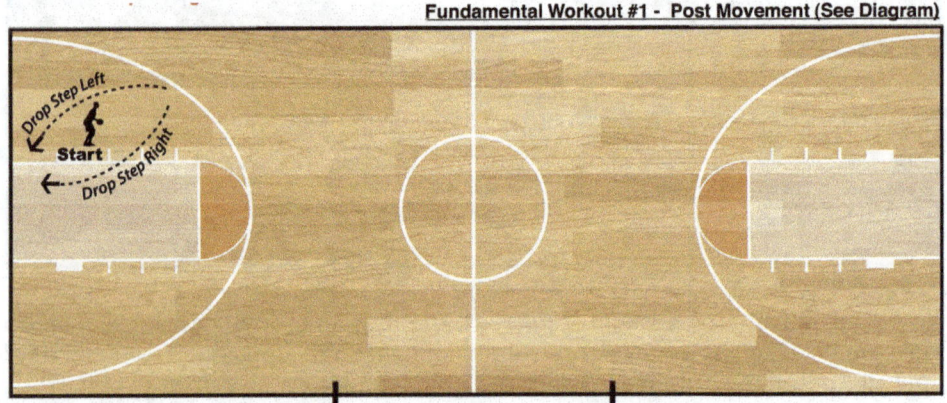

Fundamental Workout #1 - Post Movement (See Diagram)

Repeat workout until you make 5 baskets from each task listed below before moving on to a different area. Locate the starting areas on the diagram. Go as quickly as you can to get your own rebound. No dribble is needed. The sequence should go *shoot basketball, sprint to get rebound, place basketball where it should be, sprint back to starting point, and repeat movements again.* Remember no dribble is needed unless directed in a movement. In this workout always start your workout near the basket. Basketball is placed on the ground at the starting point if you are doing the workout alone and you do not have a person to pass you the ball.

Follow the sequence given below.

Fundamental Workout #1-Post Movement (See Diagram)

Start out underneath the basket on the right block.

1. Drop step (go left), jump stop & make a right hand overhand layup
2. Reverse pivot right, shot fake & make a jump shot
3. Reverse pivot right, shot fake, dribble and spin right & make a right hand overhand jump hook
4. Drop step (go right), jump stop & make a left hand jump hook
5. Reverse pivot left, shot fake & make a jump shot

See "Fundamental Workout #1 Continued-Post Movement" card

LEVEL II PERIMETER & POST FOOTWORK

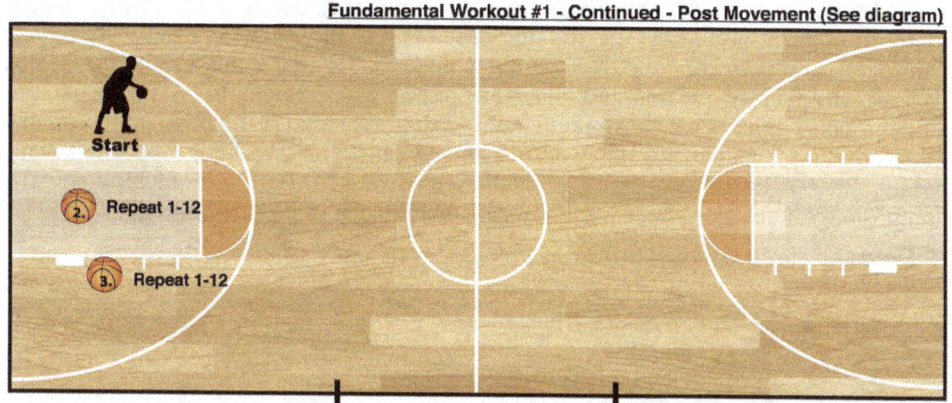

Fundamental Workout #1 Continued-Post Movement (See Diagram)

Start out underneath the basket on the right block. (make 5 baskets from each task listed below)

6. Reverse pivot left, shot fake, dribble and spin left & make a left hand overhand layup
7. Front pivot left & make a fade away jump shot
8. Front pivot left, shot fake, and make a jump hook
9. Front pivot left, shot fake, spin to the right, jump stop and make a right hand over hand layup
10. Front pivot right & make a fade away jump shot
11. Front pivot right, shot fake, and make a jump hook
12. Front pivot right, shot fake, spin to the left, jump stop and make a left hand jump hook

Move to next spot on diagram (front of rim & left block) and repeat movements above.

Water break- 5 minutes

Repeat workout until you make 3 baskets from each task listed below before moving on to different area. Locate the starting areas on the diagram. Go as quickly as you can to get your own rebound. No dribble is needed. The sequence should go - shoot basketball, sprint to get rebound, place basketball where it should be, sprint back to starting point and repeat movements again. Remember no dribble is needed unless directed in a movement. In this workout always start your workout on the left wing behind the 3 pt. line. Basketball is placed on the ground at the ending point if you are doing the workout alone and you do not have a person to pass you the ball.

Follow the sequence given below.

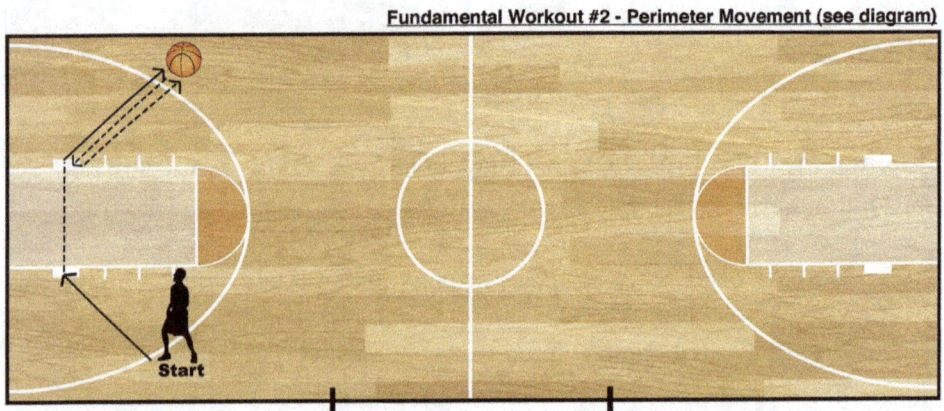

Fundamental Workout #2 - Perimeter Movement (see diagram)

Repeat workout until you make 3 baskets from each task listed below before moving on to a different area. Locate the starting areas on the diagram. Go as quickly as you can to get your own rebound. No dribble is needed. The sequence should go *shoot basketball, sprint to get rebound, place basketball where it should be, sprint back to starting point, and repeat movements again.* Remember no dribble is needed unless directed in a movement. In this workout always start your workout on the left wing behind the 3pt line. Basketball is placed on the ground at the ending point if you are doing the workout alone and you do not have a person to pass you the ball.

Follow the sequence given below.

Fundamental Workout #2-Perimeter Movement (See Diagram)

Start out on the left wing behind the 3pt line

1. Run to right wing (foot touches the left & right blocks), run back down and touch right block again, run back to right wing, pick up the basketball and make one 3 pt. jump shot
2. Run to right wing (foot touches the left & right blocks), run back down and touch right block again, run back to right wing, pick up the basketball, shot fake, (go right) 1 dribble towards the basket, and make a jump shot

See "Fundamental Workout #2 Continued-Perimeter Movement" card

LEVEL II PERIMETER & POST FOOTWORK

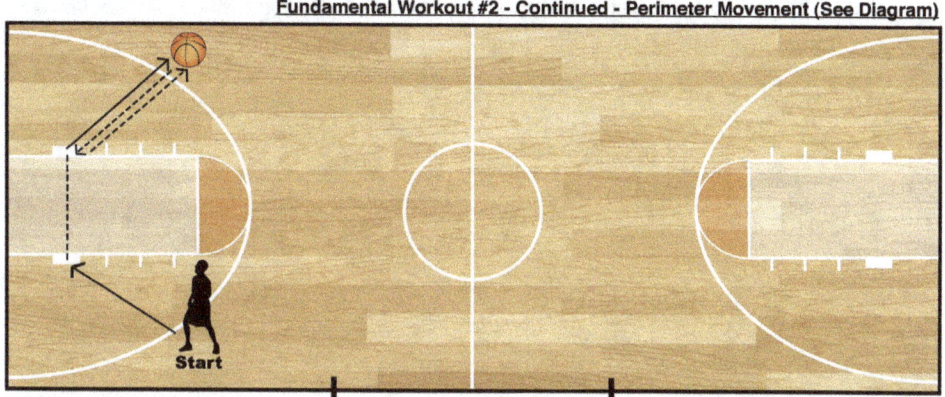

Fundamental Workout #2 Continued-Perimeter Movement (See Diagram)

Start out on the left wing behind the 3pt line

3. Run to right wing (foot touches the left & right blocks), run back down and touch right block again, run back to right wing, pick up the basketball, shot fake, (go right) 1-2 dribbles, and make a right hand overhand layup

4. Run to right wing (foot touches the left & right blocks), run back down and touch right block again, run back to right wing, pick up the basketball, shot fake, (go left) 1 dribble towards the basket, and make a jump shot

5. Run to right wing (foot touches the left & right blocks), run back down and touch right block again, run back to right wing, pick up the basketball, shot fake, (go left) 1-2 dribbles, and make a left hand overhand shot

6. Run to right elbow (go down and touch the left & right blocks first), push off with inside foot at the right elbow, run out to right wing, pick up the basketball and make 1 3pt jump shot

See "Fundamental Workout #2 Continued-1-Perimeter Movement" card

Fundamental Workout #2 Continued-2-Perimeter Movement (See Diagram)

Start out on the left wing behind the 3pt line

7. Run to right elbow (go down and touch the left & right blocks first), push off with inside foot at the right elbow, run out to right wing, pick up the basketball, shot fake, (go right) 1 dribble towards the basket, and make a jump shot

8. Run to right elbow (go down and touch the left & right blocks first), push off with inside foot at the right elbow, run out to right wing, pick up the basketball, shot fake, (go right) 1-2 dribbles, and make a right hand overhand layup

9. Run to right elbow (go down and touch the left & right blocks first), push off with inside foot at the right elbow, run out to right wing, pick up the basketball, shot fake, (go left) 1 dribble towards the basket, and make a jump shot

See "Fundamental Workout #2 Continued-2-Perimeter Movement" card

LEVEL II PERIMETER & POST FOOTWORK

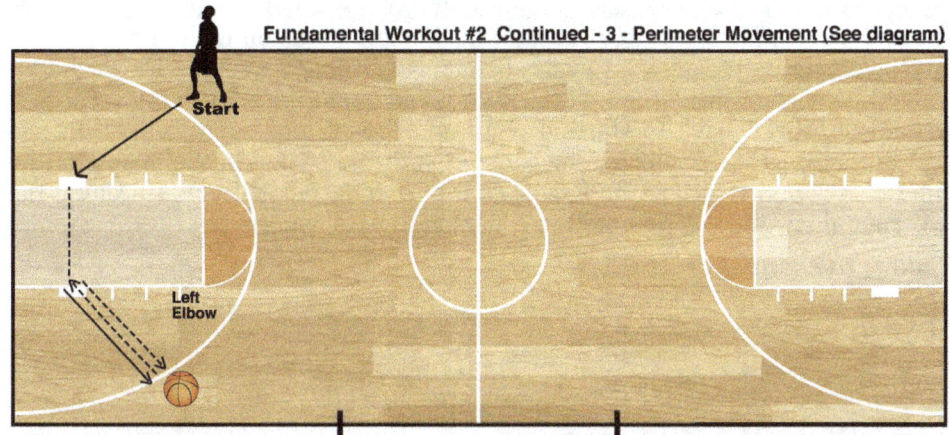

Fundamental Workout #2 Continued-3-Perimeter Movement (See Diagram)

Start out on the left wing behind the 3pt line

10. Run to right elbow (go down and touch the left & right blocks first), push off with inside foot at the right elbow, run out to right wing, pick up the basketball, shot fake, (go left) 1-2 dribbles, and make a left hand overhand shot

Move to next areas on the diagram (left wing to right wing & left wing to right elbow) and repeat movements above. Always start on wing behind the 3pt line in this workout

Water break- 5 minutes

Repeat workout until you make 5 jump shots from each task listed below before moving on to a different area. Locate the starting areas on the diagram. Go as quickly as you can to get your own rebound. No dribble is needed. The sequence should go - shoot basketball, sprint to get rebound, place basketball where it should be, sprint back to starting point and repeat movements again. In this workout always start your workout underneath the basket in the middle of the lane. Basketball is placed on the ground at ending point if you are doing the workout alone and you do not have a person to pass you the ball.

Follow the sequence given below.

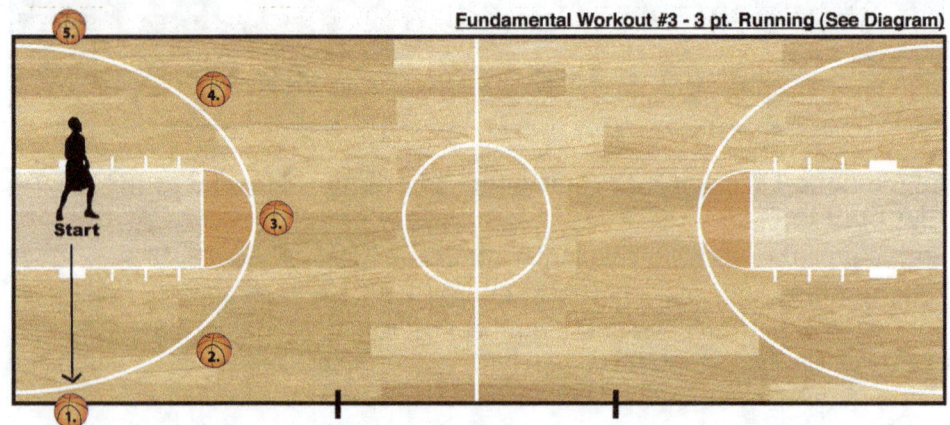

Fundamental Workout #3 - 3 pt. Running (See Diagram)

Repeat workout until you make 5 jump shots from each task listed below before moving on to a different area. Locate the starting areas on the diagram. Go as quickly as you can to get your own rebound. No dribble is needed. The sequence should go *shoot basketball, sprint to get rebound, place basketball where it should be, sprint back to starting point, and repeat movements again.* Remember no dribble is needed at any point just rebound, sprinting, and shooting. In this workout always start your workout underneath the basket in the middle of the lane. Basketball is placed on the ground at the ending point if you are doing the workout alone and you do not have a person to pass you the ball.

Follow the sequence given below.

Fundamental Workout #3- 3pt Running (See Diagram)

Start underneath the basket in the middle of the lane

1. Run out to left corner behind 3pt line, pick up the basketball and make 1 jump shot from the left 3pt corner spot
2. Run out to left wing behind 3pt line, pick up the basketball and make 1 jump shot from the left 3pt wing spot

See "Fundamental Workout #3 Continued-3pt Running" card

LEVEL II PERIMETER & POST FOOTWORK

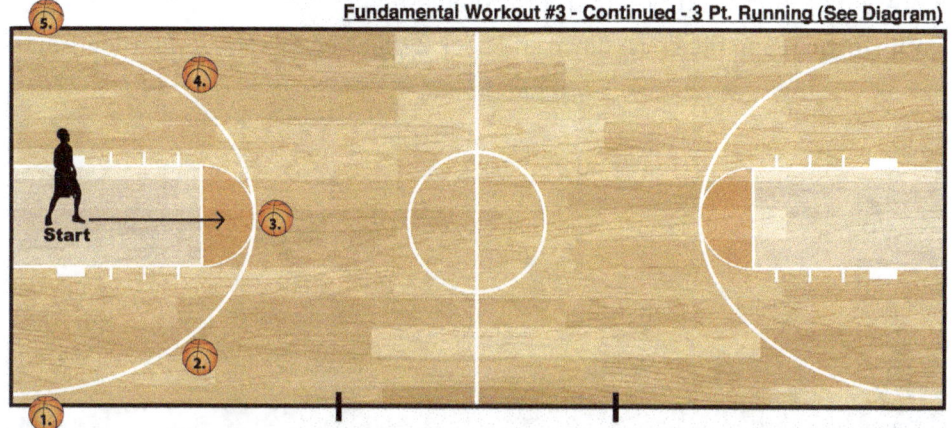

Fundamental Workout #3 Continued-3pt Running (See Diagram)

Start underneath the basket in the middle of the lane

3. Run out to the center top of key 3pt spot, pick up the basketball make 1 jump shot from the center 3pt top of key spot
4. Run out to right wing behind 3pt line, pick up the basketball and make 1 jump shot from the right 3pt wing spot
5. Run out to right corner behind 3pt line, pick up the basketball and make 1 jump shot from the right 3pt corner spot

Water break- 5 minutes

Note: All cool down workouts start at the baseline.

Cool Down - (Run full court down and back 2 times before shooting free throws)

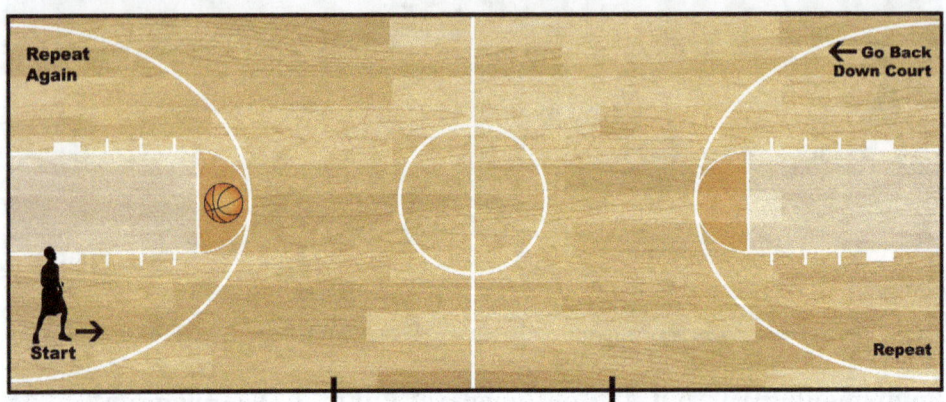

Note: All cool down workouts start at the baseline.

Cool Down-(Run full court down and back 2 times before shooting free throws)

Start on the baseline.

1. Make two (2) free throws in a row. (If you do not make the 2 free throws in a row, repeat movements in cool down listed above before trying to make 2 free throws in a row again)

Finish

Note: Perform the moves listed. Do as many repetitions as you can. Remember to warm up and rest when needed.

The B180 Basketball Fundamental Skills Program is a physically demanding workout. This is NOT for beginners or individuals with any medical condition that may be compromised by intense basketball training. Consult your physician and read the enclosed safety statement and other materials before beginning this program.

Chapter 10

B180 BASKETBALL FUNDAMENTAL SKILLS PROGRAM

Note: All warm up workouts start at the baseline. Individuals should do movements asked at the free throw line /half court line/ opposite free throw line/ opposite baseline. Then repeat workout going back to your starting point.

Warm Up (Perform each movement by itself down the court and back)

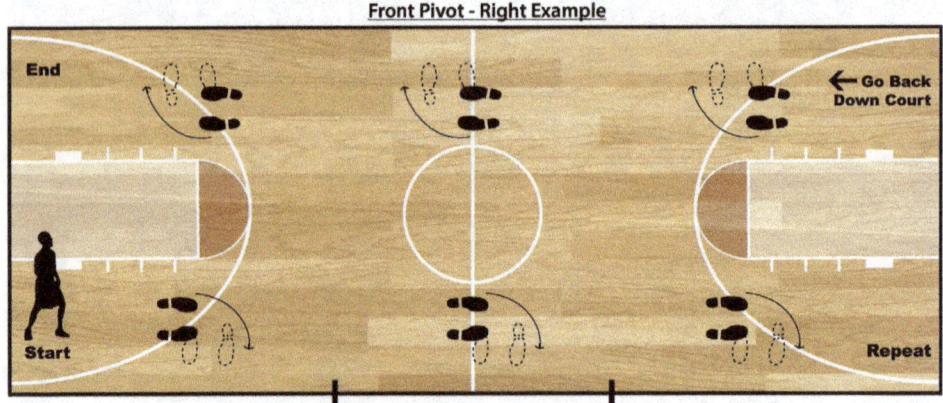

Note: All warm up workouts start at the baseline. Individuals should do movements asked at the *free throw line/half court line/ opposite free throw line/ opposite baseline.* Then repeat workout going back to your starting point.

Warm Up (perform each movement by itself down the court and back)

Jump Stop
Front Pivot Right
Front Pivot Left
Reverse Pivot Right
Reverse Pivot Left
Stutter Step
Stop and Go

Note: Perform the moves listed. Do as many repetitions as you can, then record your results after each workout. Remember to warm up and rest when needed.

The B180 Basketball Fundamental Skills Program is a physically demanding workout. This is NOT for beginners or individuals with any medical condition that may be compromised by intense basketball training. Consult your physician and read the enclosed safety statement and other materials before beginning this program.

Repeat workout for 1 minute. Follow the directions for each task listed below before moving on. Locate the starting area on the diagram. Go as quickly as you can to get to the next area on the court. Place cones at the four (4) outside 3 pt. wing areas listed on the diagram. The movement sequence should go - dribble basketball to cone, breakdown into low stance 3/4 of the way while dribbling the basketball low, slide at an angle back toward the basket, crossover and go forward, dribble to cone at the far end of the court, repeat movements again, dribble in to make a layup, go back down court repeating movements again. In this workout always start your workout on the baseline near the left corner.

Follow the sequence given below.

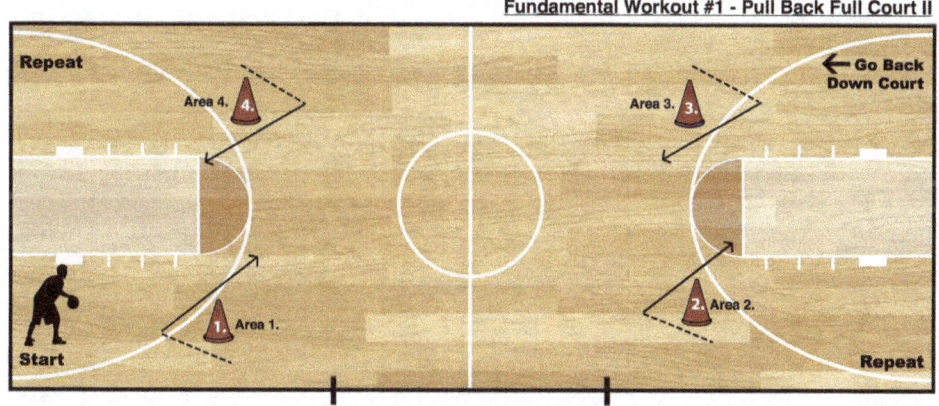

Repeat workout for 1 minute. Follow the directions for each task listed below before moving on. Locate the starting area on the diagram. Go as quickly as you can to get to the next area on the court. Place cones at the four (4) outside 3pt wing areas listed on the diagram. The movement sequence should go *dribble basketball to cone, breakdown into low stance 3/4 of the ways while dribbling the basketball low, slide at an angle back towards the basket, crossover and go forward, dribble to cone at the far end of the court, repeat movements again, dribble in to make a layup, go back down court repeating movements again.* In this workout always start your workout on the baseline near the left corner.

Follow the sequence given below.

Fundamental Workout #1-Pull Back Full Court II

Start on the baseline near the left corner
1. Run and dribble basketball with (right hand) to the cone, stay low and while facing forward, dribble back towards your starting point using 2 dribbles (left foot in front, eyes looking down court), crossover dribble the basketball in front of you. Then dribble forward down court in 4 dribbles.

2. Run and dribble basketball with (right hand) to the cone, stay low and while facing forward, dribble back towards your starting point using 2 dribbles (left foot in front, eyes looking down court), crossover dribble the basketball in front of you. Then dribble forward into the lane and make 1 overhand left hand shot.

See Fundamental Workout #1 Continued- Pull Back Full Court II- card

LEVEL II BALL HANDLING WISDOM

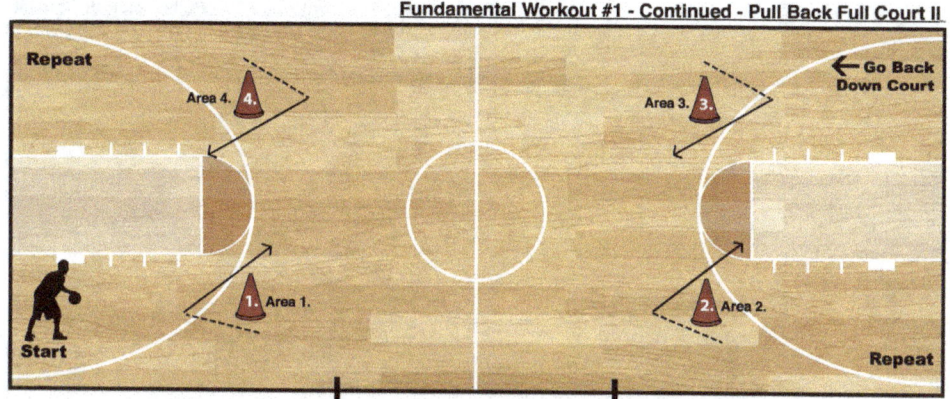

Fundamental Workout #1 Continued-Pull Back Full Court II

Start on the baseline near the left corner

3. Run and dribble basketball with (right hand) to the cone, stay low and while facing forward, dribble back towards your starting point using 2 dribbles (left foot in front, eyes looking down court), crossover dribble the basketball in front of you. Then dribble forward down court in 4 dribbles.

4. Run and dribble basketball with (right hand) to the cone, stay low and while facing forward, dribble back towards your starting point using 2 dribbles (left foot in front, eyes looking down court), crossover dribble the basketball in front of you. Then dribble forward into the lane and make 1 pull up jump shot.

Repeat movements above continuously for 1 minute going up and down both sides of the court (start in left corner at both ends of the court)

1 Minute Break

See Fundamental Workout #1 Continued-1- Pull Back Full Court II- card

Fundamental Workout #1 Continued-1-Pull Back Full Court II

Start on the baseline near the left corner

5. Run and dribble basketball with (left hand) to the cone, stay low and while facing forward, dribble back towards your starting point using 2 dribbles (right foot in front, eyes looking down court), crossover dribble the basketball in front of you. Then dribble forward down court in 4 dribbles.

6. Run and dribble basketball with (left hand) to the cone, stay low and while facing forward, dribble back towards your starting point using 2 dribbles (right foot in front, eyes looking down court), crossover dribble the basketball in front of you. Then dribble forward and make 1 overhand right hand layup.

Repeat movements above continuously for 1 minute going up and down both sides of the court (start in left corner at both ends of the court)

1 minute break

See "Fundamental Workout #1 Continued-2-Pull Back Full Court II" card

Fundamental Workout #1 Continued-2-Pull Back Full Court II

Start on the baseline near the left corner

7. Run and dribble basketball with (left hand) to the cone, stay low and while facing forward, dribble back towards your starting point using 2 dribbles (right foot in front, eyes looking down court), crossover dribble the basketball in front of you. Then dribble forward down court in 4 dribbles.

8. Run and dribble basketball with (left hand) to the cone, stay low and while facing forward, dribble back towards your starting point using 2 dribbles (right foot in front, eyes looking down court), crossover dribble the basketball in front of you. Then dribble forward and make 1 pull up jump shot.

**Repeat all movements above while starting in right corner near baseline. You will have 4 (1 minute) segments left. They are starting with

1. right hand dribble down and back for 1 minute-layup
2. right hand dribble down and back for 1 minute-pull up jump shot
3. left hand dribble down and back for 1 minute-layup
4. left hand dribble down and back for 1 minute-pull up jump shot

Water break- 5 minutes

Locate the starting areas on the diagram. Go as quick as you can. In this workout always start your workout on the baseline.

Follow the sequence given below.

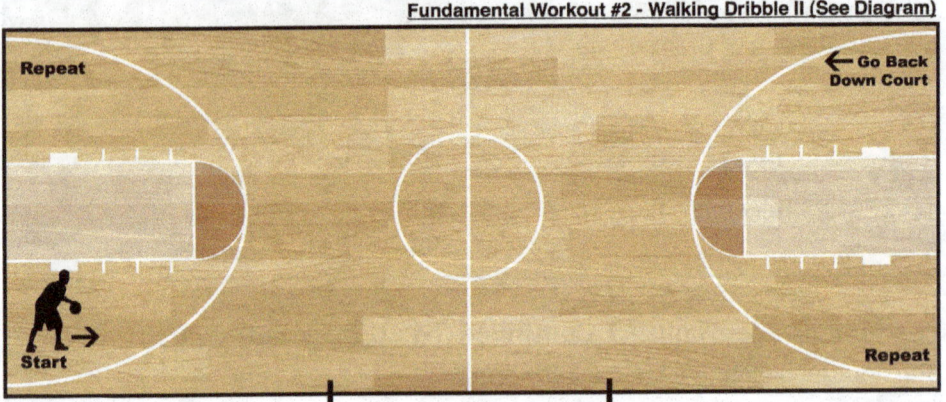

Locate the starting areas on the diagram. Go as quick as you can. In this workout always start your workout on the baseline.

Follow the sequence given below.

Fundamental Workout #2- Walking Dribble II (See Diagram)

Start on the baseline

1. Walk down court and dribble between the leg continuously (alternating with left & right hand). Dribble 100 times between the leg without mishandling the basketball or losing your dribble. Go down the court and back

2. Walk down court and dribble (right hand). Stay low to the ground and dribble between the legs and then crossover with your left hand in front of you. Do these movements continuously 100 times between leg and crossover without mishandling the basketball or losing your dribble. Go down the court and back

3. Walk down court and dribble (left hand). Stay low to the ground and dribble between the legs and then crossover with your right hand in front of you. Do these movements continuously 100 times between leg and crossover without mishandling the basketball or losing your dribble. Go down the court and back

See "Fundamental Workout #2 Continued-Walking Dribble II" card

LEVEL II BALL HANDLING WISDOM

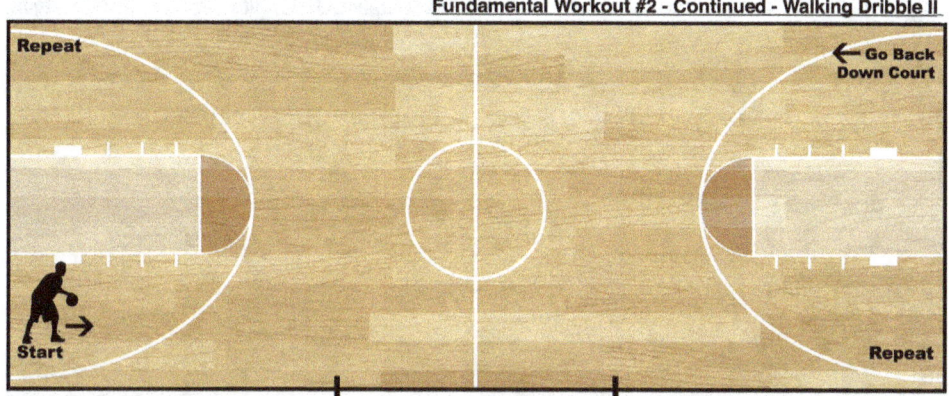

Fundamental Workout #2 - Continued - Walking Dribble II

Fundamental Workout #2 Continued-Walking Dribble II

Start on the baseline

4. Walk down court and dribble (right hand). Stay low to the ground and dribble between the legs and then go behind your back with your left hand. Do these movements continuously 100 times between leg and behind the back without mishandling the basketball or losing your dribble. Go down the court and back

5. Walk down court and dribble (left hand). Stay low to the ground and dribble between the legs and then go behind your back with your right hand. Do these movements continuously 100 times between leg and behind the back without mishandling the basketball or losing your dribble. Go down the court and back

6. Walk down court and dribble (right hand). Stay low to the ground and dribble between the legs and then do a spin move while the ball is in our left hand. Do these movements 4 times down the court. Go down the court and back

7. Walk down court and dribble (left hand). Stay low to the ground and dribble between the legs and then do a spin move while the ball is in our right hand. Do these movements 4 times down the court. Go down the court and back

See Fundamental Workout # 2 Continued-1- Walking Dribble II- card

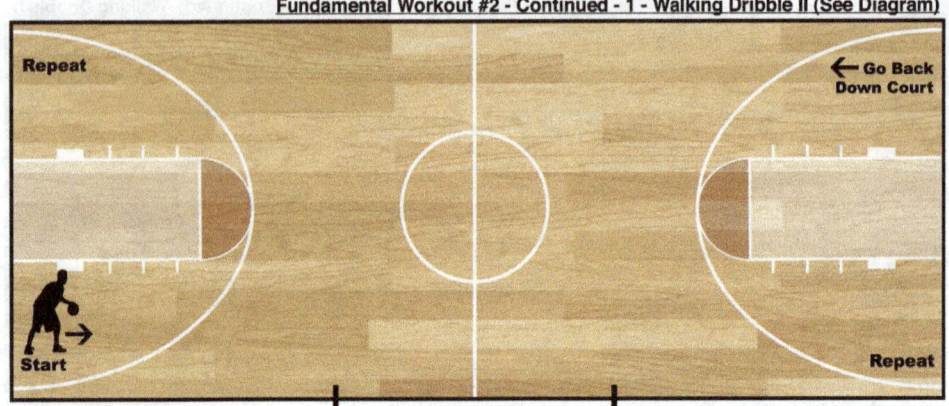

Fundamental Workout #2 Continued-1- Walking Dribble II (See Diagram)

Start on the baseline

8. Walk down court and dribble (right hand). Stay low to the ground and dribble moving the ball in and out in a circle motion (hand stays on top of the basketball). Do these movements continuously 100 times in and out without mishandling the basketball or losing your dribble. Go down the court and back

9. Walk down court and dribble (left hand). Stay low to the ground and dribble moving the ball in and out in a circle motion (hand stays on top of the basketball). Do these movements continuously 100 times in and out without mishandling the basketball or losing your dribble. Go down the court and back

10. Walk down court and dribble two (2) basketballs. Stay low to the ground and crossover dribble the basketballs in front of you. Do these movements 5 times down the court. Go down the court and back

11. Walk down court and dribble three (3) basketballs. Stay low to the ground and crossover dribble the basketballs in front of you (push 1 of the basketball slightly out in front of you while dribbling the other two). Do these movements 5 times down the court. Go down the court and back

Water Break- 5 Minutes

LEVEL II BALL HANDLING WISDOM

Repeat workout until 3 shots in a row are made from each task listed below. Follow the directions for each task listed below before moving on. Locate the starting area on the diagram. Go as quickly as you can to get to the next area on the court. Place cones at the three (3) outside 3 pt. areas listed on the diagram. The movement sequence should go - dribble basketball into the lane, breakdown into low stance 3/4 of the way, while dribbling the basketball low, slide at an angle back towards the 3 pt. line, crossover and go forward, dribble in to make 1 shot, go back to the 3 pt. area repeating movements again. In this workout always start your workout on the right wing behind the 3 pt. line.

Follow the sequence given below.

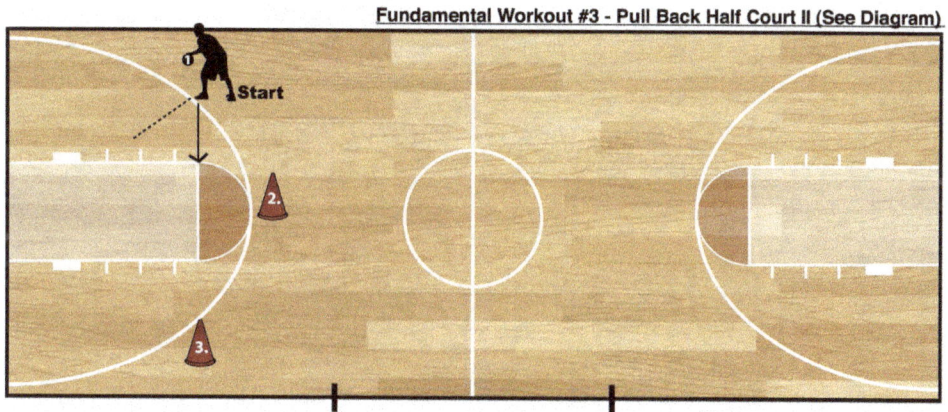

Fundamental Workout #3 - Pull Back Half Court II (See Diagram)

Repeat workout until 3 shots in a row are made from each task listed below. Follow the directions for each task listed below before moving on. Locate the starting area on the diagram. Go as quickly as you can to get to the next area on the court. Place cones at the three (3) outside 3pt areas listed on the diagram. The movement sequence should go *dribble basketball into the lane, breakdown into low stance 3/4 of the ways while dribbling the basketball low, slide at an angle back towards the 3pt line, crossover and go forward, dribble in to make 1 shot, go back to 3 pt area repeating movements again.* In this workout always start your workout on the right wing behind the 3 pt. line.

Follow the sequence given below.

Fundamental Workout #3-Pull Back Half Court II (See Diagram)

Start on the right wing behind the 3pt line

1. Run and dribble basketball twice with (right hand) towards the right block, make a pull up jump shot
2. Run and dribble basketball with (right hand) towards the right block, stay low and while facing forward, dribble back towards your starting point using 2 dribbles (left foot in front, eyes looking up at the basket), crossover dribble the basketball in front of you. Then dribble forward towards the lane and make 1 elbow jump shot

3. Run and dribble basketball with (right hand) towards the right block, stay low and while facing forward, dribble back towards your starting point using 2 dribbles (left foot in front, eyes looking up at the basket), crossover dribble the basketball in front of you. Then dribble forward into the lane and make 1 overhand left hand shot

See Fundamental Workout #3 Continued-Pull Back Half Court II- card

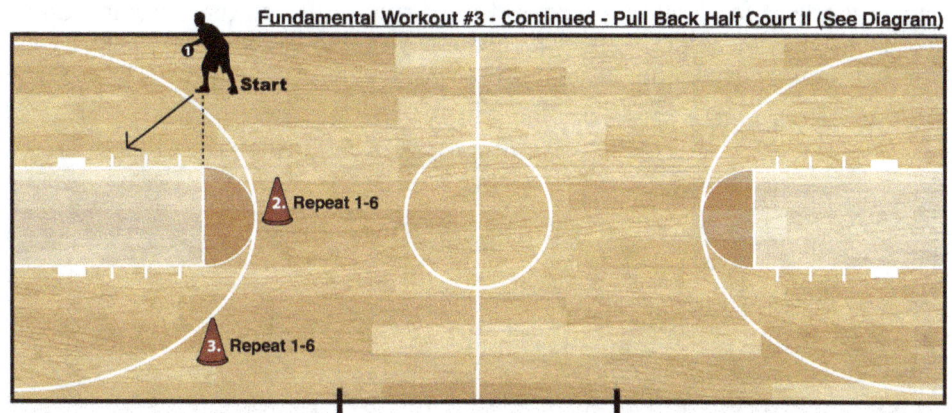

Fundamental Workout #3 Continued- Pull Back Half Court II (See Diagram)

Start on the right wing behind the 3pt line- (Make 3 shots in a row from each task listed below)

4. Run and dribble basketball twice with (left hand) towards the inside lane area, make a pull up jump shot
5. Run and dribble basketball with (left hand) towards the inside lane area, stay low and while facing forward, dribble back towards your starting point using 2 dribbles (right foot in front, eyes looking up at the basket), crossover dribble the basketball in front of you. Then dribble forward towards the right block and make 1 jump shot near the short corner
6. Run and dribble basketball with (left hand) towards the inside lane area, stay low and while facing forward, dribble back towards your starting point using 2 dribbles (right foot in front, eyes looking up at the basket), crossover dribble the basketball in front of you. Then dribble forward towards the right block and make 1 overhand right hand layup

Move to next spot on diagram and repeat movements above. The next areas would be

1. top of key behind 3pt line
2. left wing area behind 3pt line

Water Break- 5 minutes

Repeat workout for 1 minute. Locate the starting areas on the diagram. Go as quickly as you can to get your own rebound. In this workout always start your workout on the baseline underneath the basket.

Follow the sequence given below.

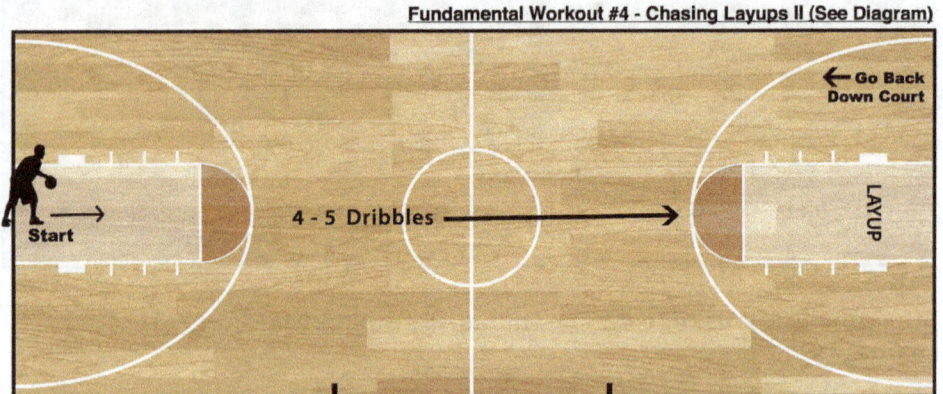

Repeat workout for 1 minute. Locate the starting areas on the diagram. Go as quickly as you can to get your own rebound. In this workout always start your workout on the baseline underneath the basket.

Follow the sequence given below.

Fundamental Workout #4-Chasing Layups II (See Diagram)

Start on the baseline

1. Run while dribbling (alternate left & right hand) the basketball using 4-5 dribbles down court to the other basket and make a right hand overhand layup. Get your rebound
2. Run while dribbling (alternate left & right hand) the basketball using 4-5 dribbles down court to the other basket and make a right hand overhand layup. Get your rebound

Repeat movements for 1 minute

1 minute break

3. Run while dribbling (alternate left & right hand) the basketball using 4-5 dribbles down court to the other basket and make a left hand overhand layup. Get your rebound
4. Run while dribbling (alternate left & right hand) the basketball using 4-5 dribbles down court to the other basket and make a left hand overhand layup. Get your rebound

Repeat movement for 1 minute

See Fundamental Workout #4 Continued- Chasing Layups II- card

LEVEL II BALL HANDLING WISDOM

Fundamental Workout #4 - Continued - Chasing Layups II (See Diagram)

Fundamental Workout #4 Continued- Chasing Layups II (See Diagram)

Start on the baseline

5. Run while dribbling (alternate left & right hand) the basketball using 4-5 dribbles down court to the other basket and make a pull up free throw line jump shot. Get your rebound
6. Run while dribbling (alternate left & right hand) the basketball using 4-5 dribbles down court to the other basket and make a pull up free throw line jump shot. Get your rebound

Repeat movements for 1 minute

1 minute break

7. Run while dribbling (alternate left & right hand) the basketball using 4-5 dribbles down court to the other basket and make a pull up center top of key 3pt jump shot. Get your rebound
8. Run while dribbling (alternate left & right hand) the basketball using 4-5 dribbles down court to the other basket and make a pull up center top of key 3pt jump shot. Get your rebound

Repeat movements for 1 minute

Water break- 5 minutes

<u>Repeat workout until you make 1 shot from each task listed below</u>. Locate the five (5) starting areas behind the 3 pt. line on diagram. Go as quickly as you can to get your own rebound. In this workout always start your workout behind 3 point line.

Follow the sequence given below.

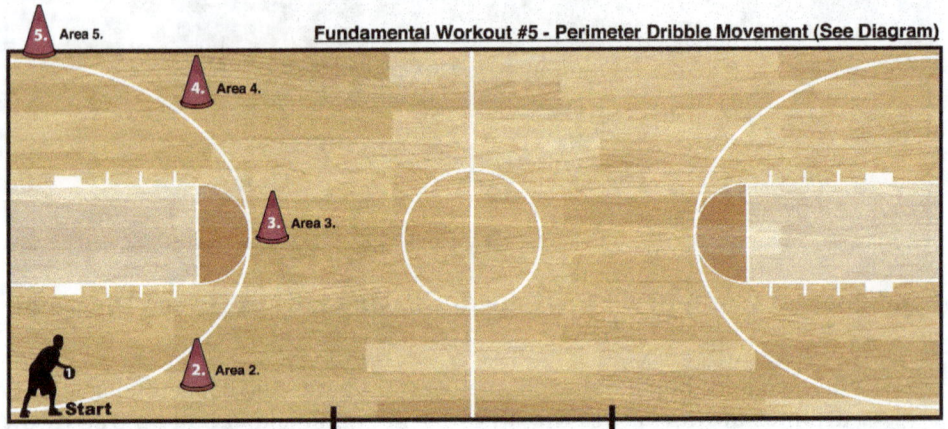

<u>Repeat workout until you make 1 shot from each task listed below.</u> Locate the five (5) starting areas behind the 3pt line on diagram. Go as quickly as you can to get your own rebound. In this workout always start your workout behind three point line.

Follow the sequence given below.

Fundamental Workout #5-Perimeter Dribble Movement (See Diagram)

Start in the left corner behind 3pt line

1. Dribble (right hand) the basketball low to the ground. Do a between the leg crossover dribble from right to left hand. Perform 1-2 dribbles towards the basket (go left). Make a pull up jump shot
2. Dribble (right hand) the basketball low to the ground. Do a between the leg crossover dribble from right to left hand. Perform 1-2 dribbles towards the basket (go left). Make an overhand left hand layup
3. Dribble (left hand) the basketball low to the ground. Do a between the leg crossover dribble from left to right hand. Perform 1-2 dribbles towards the basket (go right). Make a pull up jump shot
4. Dribble (left hand) the basketball low to the ground. Do a between the leg crossover dribble from left to right hand. Perform 1-2 dribbles towards the basket (go right). Make an overhand right hand layup

See Fundamental Workout #5 Continued- Perimeter Dribble Movement- card

LEVEL II BALL HANDLING WISDOM

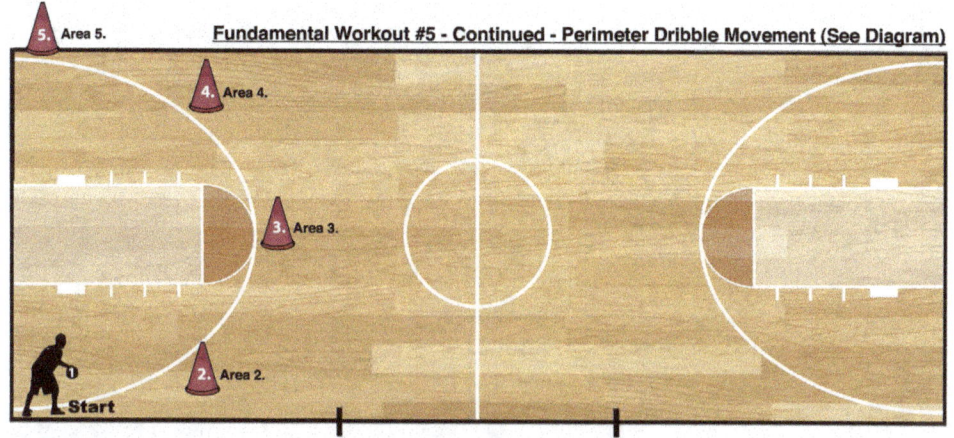

Fundamental Workout #5 Continued- Perimeter Dribble Movement (See Diagram)

Start in the left corner behind 3pt line

5. Dribble (right hand) the basketball low to the ground. <u>Do a between the leg behind the back dribble from right to left hand. Perform 1-2 dribbles towards the basket (go right)</u>. Make a pull up jump shot

6. Dribble (right hand) the basketball low to the ground. <u>Do a between the leg behind the back dribble from right to left hand. Perform 1-2 dribbles towards the basket (go right)</u>. Make an overhand left hand layup

7. Dribble (left hand) the basketball low to the ground. <u>Do a between the leg behind the back dribble from left to right hand. Perform 1-2 dribbles towards the basket (go left)</u>. Make a pull up jump shot

8. Dribble (left hand) the basketball low to the ground. <u>Do a between the leg behind the back dribble from left to right hand. Perform 1-2 dribbles towards the basket (go left)</u>. Make an overhand left hand layup

See Fundamental Workout #5 Continued-1- Perimeter Dribble Movement- card

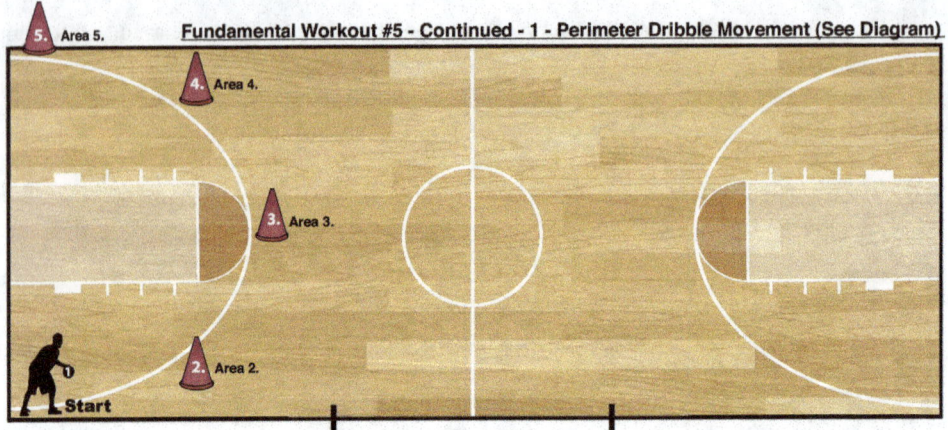

Fundamental Workout #5 Continued-1-Perimeter Dribble Movement (See Diagram)

Start in the left corner behind 3pt line

9. Dribble (right hand) the basketball low to the ground. <u>Do an In & Out dribble. Perform 1-2 dribbles towards the basket (go right)</u>. Make a pull up jump shot
10. Dribble (right hand) the basketball low to the ground. <u>Do an In & Out dribble. Perform 1-2 dribbles towards the basket (go right)</u>. Make an overhand right hand layup
11. Dribble (left hand) the basketball low to the ground. <u>Do an In & Out dribble. Perform 1-2 dribbles towards the basket (go left)</u>. Make a pull up jump shot
12. Dribble (left hand) the basketball low to the ground. <u>Do an In & Out dribble. Perform 1-2 dribbles towards the basket (go left)</u>. Make an overhand left hand layup

Move to next spots on diagram and repeat movements above. They are:

1. Left wing behind the 3pt line
2. Top of key behind the 3pt line
3. Right wing behind the 3pt line
4. Right corner behind the 3pt line

Water Break- 5 minutes

LEVEL II BALL HANDLING WISDOM

Note: All cool down workouts start at the baseline.

Cool Down - (Run full court down and back 2 times before shooting free throws)

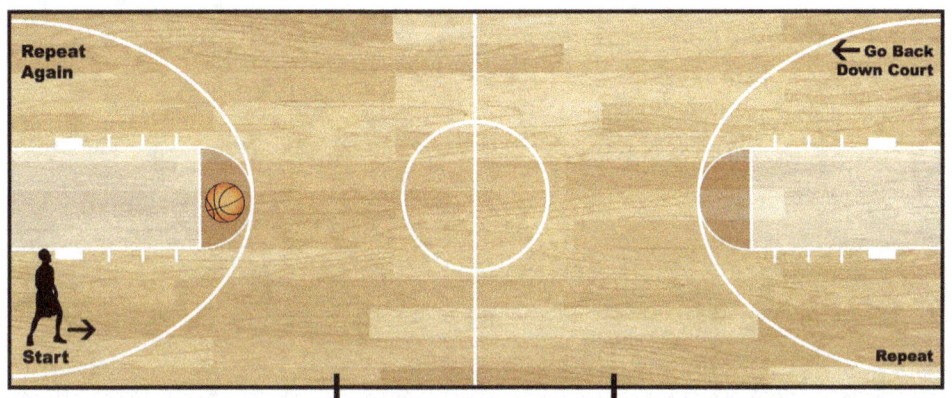

Note: All cool down workouts start at the baseline.

Cool Down-(Run full court down and back 2 times before shooting free throws)

Start on the baseline.

1. Make two (2) free throws in a row. (If you do not make the 2 free throws in a row, repeat movements in cool down listed above before trying to make 2 free throws in a row again)

Finish

Note: Perform the moves listed. Do as many repetitions as you can. Remember to warm up and rest when needed.

The B180 Basketball Fundamental Skills Program is a physically demanding workout. This is NOT for beginners or individuals with any medical condition that may be compromised by intense basketball training. Consult your physician and read the enclosed safety statement and other materials before beginning this program.

Chapter 11

LEVEL II PURE SHOOTING

Note: All warm up workouts start at the baseline. Individuals should do movements asked at the free throw line /half court line/ opposite free throw line/ opposite baseline. Then repeat workout going back to your starting point.

Warm Up (Perform each movement by itself down the court and back)

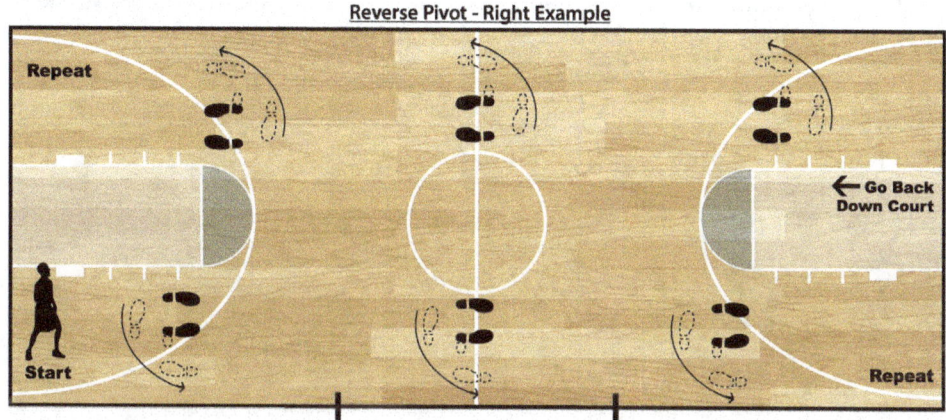

Note: All warm up workouts start at the baseline. Individuals should do movements asked at the *free throw line/half court line/ opposite free throw line/ opposite baseline.* Then repeat workout going back to your starting point.

Warm Up (perform each movement by itself down the court and back)

Jump Stop
Front Pivot Right
Front Pivot Left
Reverse Pivot Right
Reverse Pivot Left
Stutter Step
Stop and Go

Note: Perform the moves listed. Do as many repetitions as you can, then record your results after each workout. Remember to warm up and rest when needed.

The B180 Basketball Fundamental Skills Program is a physically demanding workout. This is NOT for beginners or individuals with any medical condition that may be compromised by intense basketball training. Consult your physician and read the enclosed safety statement and other materials before beginning this program.

Repeat workout until you make 15 jump shots from each task listed below before moving on to a different area. Locate the starting areas on the diagram. Go as quickly as you can to get your own rebound. No dribble is needed. The sequence should go - shoot basketball, sprint to get rebound, sprint back to area with the basketball and shoot the basketball again. Remember no dribble is needed at any point just rebound, sprint and shoot. In this workout always start your workout near the basket.

Follow sequence given below.

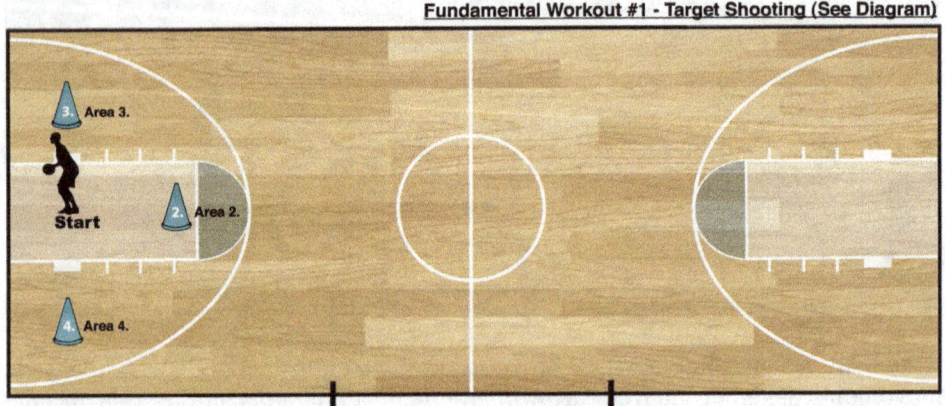

Fundamental Workout #1 - Target Shooting (See Diagram)

Repeat workout until you make 15 jump shots from each task listed below before moving on to a different area. Locate the starting areas on the diagram. Go as quickly as you can to get your own rebound. No dribble is needed. The sequence should go *shoot basketball, sprint to get rebound, sprint back to area with the basketball and shoot the basketball again*. Remember no dribble is needed at any point just rebound, sprinting, and shooting. In this workout always start your workout near the basket.

Follow the sequence given below.

Fundamental Workout #1-Target Shooting (See Diagram)

Start out underneath the basket between the right and left blocks in the middle of the lane.

1. Make 15 jump shots between the low post areas (shooting your normal jump shot)
2. Make 15 jump shots between the high post areas (below the left & right elbows)
3. Make 15 jump shots from the right short corner area
4. Make 15 jump shots from the left short corner area
5. Make 15 jump shots from the right elbow

See "Fundamental Workout #1 Continued-Target Shooting" card

LEVEL II PURE SHOOTING

Fundamental Workout #1- Continued-Target Shooting (See Diagram)

Start out underneath the basket between the right and left blocks in the middle of the lane.

6. Make 15 jump shots from the left elbow
7. Make 15 jump shots from the free throw line
8. Make 15 right hand layups starting from the right elbow (use 1 dribble)
9. Make 15 left hand layups starting from the left elbow (use 1 dribble)

Move to 3pt areas listed on diagram and repeat movements above.

Water break- 5 minutes

Repeat workout until you make 3 jump shots in a row from each task listed below before moving on to a different area. Locate the starting areas on the diagram. Go as quickly as you can to get your own rebound. No dribble is needed. The sequence should go – shoot basketball, sprint to get rebound, sprint back to area with the basketball and shoot the basketball again. Remember no dribble is needed at any point just rebound, sprint and shoot. In this workout always start your workout near the basket.

Follow the sequence given below.

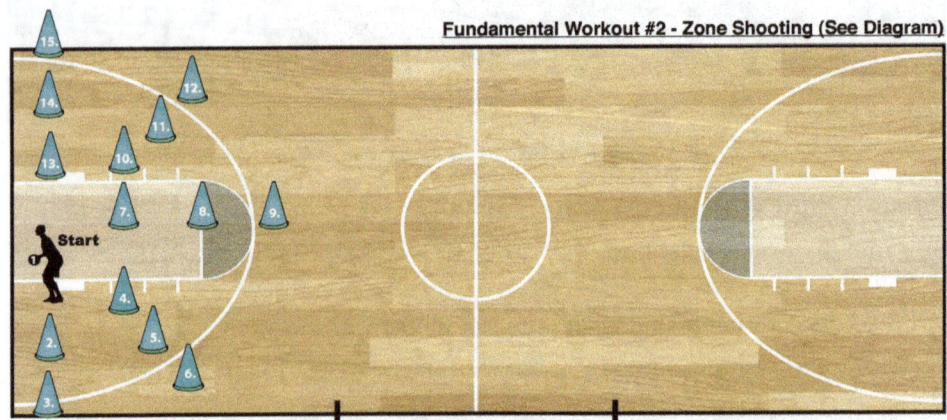

Fundamental Workout #2 - Zone Shooting (See Diagram)

Repeat workout until you make 3 jump shots in a row from each task listed below before moving on to a different area. Locate the starting areas on the diagram. Go as quickly as you can to get your own rebound. No dribble is needed. The sequence should go *shoot basketball, sprint to get rebound, sprint back to area with the basketball and shoot the basketball again.*

Remember no dribble is needed at any point just rebound, sprinting, and shooting. In this workout always start your workout near the basket.

Follow the sequence given below.

Fundamental Workout #2-Zone Shooting (See Diagram)

Start out near the basket on the left block

1. Make 3 jump shots in a row from the left block
2. Make 3 jump shots in a row from the left short corner
3. Make 3 jump shots in a row from the left corner 3pt area

Move to next areas on the diagram and repeat movements above. Always start near the basket.

Water break- 5 minutes

LEVEL II PURE SHOOTING

Repeat workout until you make 1 0 jump shots from each task listed below before moving on to a different area. Locate the starting areas on the diagram. Go as quickly as you can to get your own rebound. No dribble is needed. The sequence should go - shoot basketball, sprint to get rebound, sprint back to area with the basketball and shoot the basketball again. Remember no dribble is needed at any point just rebound, sprint and shoot. In this workout always start your workout behind the 3 pt. line.

Follow the sequence given below.

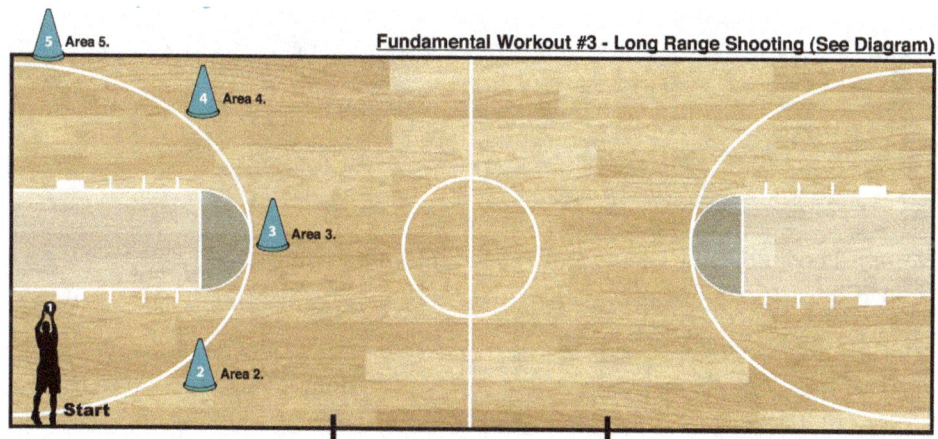

Repeat workout until you make 10 jump shots from each task listed below before moving on to a different area. Locate the starting areas on the diagram. Go as quickly as you can to get your own rebound. No dribble is needed. The sequence should go shoot basketball, sprint to get rebound, sprint back to area with the basketball and shoot the basketball again. Remember no dribble is needed at any point just rebound, sprinting, and shooting. In this workout always start your workout outside the 3pt line.

Follow the sequence given below.

Fundamental Workout #3-Long Range Shooting (See Diagram)

Start outside the 3pt line in the left corner

1. Make 10 jump shots from the left 3pt corner spot
2. Make 10 jump shots from the left 3pt wing spot
3. Make 10 jump shots from the center 3pt top of key spot
4. Make 10 jump shots from the right 3pt wing spot
5. Make 10 jump shots from the right 3pt corner spot

Note: All cool down workouts start at the baseline.

Cool Down - (Run full court down and back 2 times before shooting free throws)

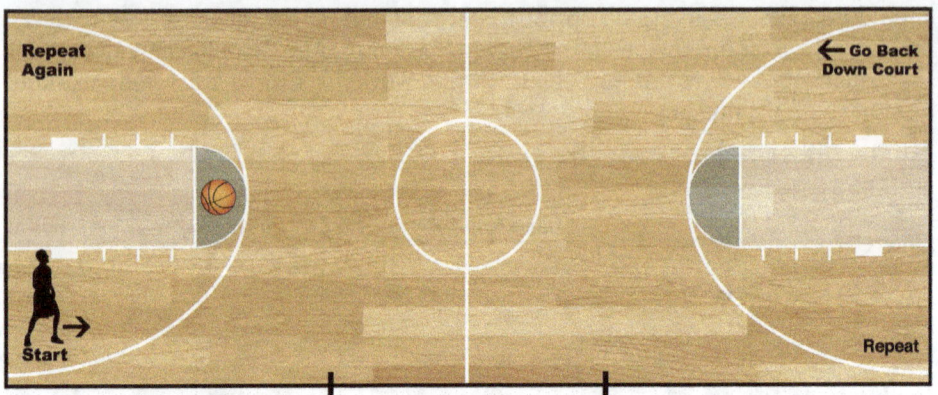

Note: All cool down workouts start at the baseline.

Cool Down-(Run full court down and back 2 times before shooting free throws)

Start on the baseline.

1. Make two (2) free throws in a row. (If you do not make the 2 free throws in a row, repeat movements in cool down listed above before trying to make 2 free throws in a row again)

Finish

Note: Perform the moves listed. Do as many repetitions as you can. Remember to warm up and rest when needed.

The B180 Basketball Fundamental Skills Program is a physically demanding workout. This is NOT for beginners or individuals with any medical condition that may be compromised by intense basketball training. Consult your physician and read the enclosed safety statement and other materials before beginning this program.

NOTES

NOTES

NOTES

NOTES

NOTES

NOTES

NOTES

NOTES

NOTES

NOTES

NOTES

NOTES

NOTES

www.ingramcontent.com/pod-product-compliance
Lightning Source LLC
Chambersburg PA
CBHW072336300426
44109CB00042B/1635